CLAUDE MONET
AND HIS GARDEN

Portrait of Monet, aged 35, by Renoir
From the Louvre

CLAUDE MONET

and his garden

The Story of an Artist's Paradise

by

Stephen Gwynn

Illustrated from photographs and
with reproductions of paintings

NEW YORK

The Macmillan Company

FIRST PUBLISHED 1934
CHEAP EDITION 1935

MADE AND PRINTED IN GREAT BRITAIN

To H. G.

T HERE IS a great literature of the Impressionist movement, and Monet himself, as was natural, received concentrated attention. A brilliant critical essay by M. Camille Mauclair in the *Maîtres de l'Art Moderne* appeared in 1924, before Monet's death. This is available in English, with forty reproductions of the artist's work. Two years earlier Gustave Geffroy had published his large volume, *Claude Monet, sa Vie, son Temps et son Œuvre*, admirably illustrated and in every way a noble and informing tribute.

La Vie de Claude Monet by Madame de Fels (in the series *Vies des Hommes Illustres*) is biography pure and simple, rather than criticism, and excellently done. Clemenceau's book, *Claude Monet, Les Nymphéas*, is in a class by itself, a vivid personal appreciation of Monet the man, and of Monet the painter. It needs to be supplemented by certain pages in the *Life* of Clemenceau himself, in which M. Georges Suarez tells even more of the relation between these two great men.

I am indebted to Sir Evan Charteris's book on John Sargent for some interesting criticism of Monet, and for a description of the man in his extreme old age.

My gratitude is due also to Sir Robert Witt for access to his great collection of photographs, and even more to M. Durand Ruel, at whose gallery on the Avenue de Friedland I was not only permitted to consult twelve albums full of photographs of Monet's work, but also to use any of them I chose.

Finally, for myself and for the publisher of *Country Life*, I must acknowledge the great kindness of Mme Blanche Monet, by whose permission direct photographs of Monet's garden have for the first time been made.

S. G.

CONTENTS

ix

LIST OF ILLUSTRATIONS

LIST OF ILLUSTRATIONS

CLAUDE MONET
AND HIS GARDEN

CHAPTER I

INTRODUCTORY

IN THE garden of the Tuileries, facing the Place de la Concorde, stands the Orangerie, now a picture gallery, like its pendant at the opposite corner, the Jeu de Paume. Two great rooms in it, below the ground level and lighted only from the top, are devoted to the display of Claude Monet's bequest to his nation. There are eight of these pictures, set in the walls between the openings so as to make a continuous band of panelling; and they are on a vast scale; one of them fifty feet from side to side, none less than half as long. All are pictures of a garden, pictures of the same garden, pictures of Claude Monet's garden, which he devised, created, and watched over during the last forty years of his long life; and which by his testament is maintained to-day in the same order and disposition as he left it.

The pictures are there in Paris for all the world to see; they have been there ever since Monet died in 1926—a patriarch of his art, who till death could never be brought to part from this his final work— never sure that the utmost had been done that he could do. There they will remain, the lasting possession of France, held in trust for all lovers of beauty, and of a genius that had its own most individual way of seeing beauty. Just as pictures, they must be known to tens of thousands. But—if I may be allowed to say why this book came to be written—it was the fortune of my ignorance, before I saw these paintings or knew of their existence, to stumble, under happy guidance, on the garden that inspired them, at a moment when its characteristic glory was in full bloom.

It was one of those enchanting surprises which will set the least sensitive mind to work; and from the garden I made my way, of course, to the Orangerie; but I was led also to track out the story of the paintings, which is indeed the story of Claude Monet's life, an extreme, typical and most noble example of an artist's career. For it begins with the sudden, almost mystical, discovery of a vocation, and passes on through years of passionate study, leading at first to penury and neglect (to which in this case derision was added abundantly), but finally to the gradual attainment of success, reputation, a handsome competence. Yet it never records an abandonment of effort. To the last, even when the cruellest physical disabilities were added, this follower of a vision strove after the unattainable perfection, seeking to fix on canvas the very spirit of that beauty which shifts and changes as you watch.

An artist's nature is revealed in his works, and, by

The Pond from the East

the consent of all who have written about him, Monet's garden ranks among his most characteristic creations. Nothing could be a completer image of tranquillity than this pool of water, enclosed by drooping willows, with many-coloured lilies afloat on the surface. Yet in the paintings of it which he has given to the nation, that still mirror reflects a passionate world, charged with colour, pulsating with vital movement. For with him, external tranquillity was only the condition making possible an inner life of endless effort.

The story when I learnt it told me how this peaceable solitary had been a rebel in the domain of his art, steadily, at all costs, refusing submission to conventions; going his own way, till at last the world followed him; till the name of Impressionists—invented from the title of one of Monet's pictures, and fixed in derision on a little group—became recognised as the distinctive mark of those who had given to France new leadership in the world of art. Monet did not stand alone; but for his essential achievement he owed nothing to anyone. France and the world owed more to him than to any other painter of his time; and it was only after he had conquered his material tranquillity, after he was able to create for himself this environment of beauty, this refuge for meditation which was in itself inspiration and stimulus, that he gave the full measure of his passionate art.

CLAUDE MONET *and* HIS GARDEN

In his house at Giverny, when I first entered the room, hung with sketches of his pictures, where he used to work, my eye was fascinated by a photograph of a benign and charming patriarch. It was a perfect example of what the camera can do when skilfully directed; and in this case, Sacha Guitry, playwright, poet and actor, had been the photographer. But Monet's own portrait of himself, hung outside the oval rooms at the Orangerie, shows an old face congested with passion. It shows the artist flushed with successful effort; but it shows also the man who after days and weeks of labour would as often as not drive his boot through the canvas.

There is another way of knowing a man than by his works. *Noscitur a sociis*; his intimates stamp him; and nothing so much surprised me, when I sought details of Monet's, as to find by whom the story was most intimately told. It was Georges Clemenceau, no lesser man, who, after he had seen the burial of his friend and contemporary, felt the impulse to describe a life whose progress he had watched for more than sixty years. He was in his right. When both men were over seventy, the old politician, journalist, duellist, writer, philosopher, statesman, grown grey in a thousand turmoils and controversies, kept pressing the painter, sedentary in that peaceful village by the Seine where the Ile de France passes into Normandy, to complete his life's work with a heroic gesture. Since the French State had

4

never bought a canvas from him, never honoured him with so much as a ribbon, he should enrich his country with the gift of work into which, as it were, the distilled essence of his genius had been poured.

Nothing is lacking to complete the drama of this alliance. By 1914 Clemenceau's persuasion had triumphed over Monet's unwillingness; for in part he was loath to offer a gift which in itself must imply great assurance of established fame, but still more doubtful of his power to grapple in old age with that interplay of textures, shapes and shades, where liquid and solid in their contact and fusion offered problems whose complexity no painter could ignore: and how much more complicated were they to the eye that had found a bewildering range of vibrant tones in a single sunlit haystack! Yet the decision was taken; and then came the crash of war. Nothing is perhaps more characteristic of Monet, whose will to an end was always single and unshakeable, than that this altered nothing for him, except by imposing delay. Of all years, it was in 1916, when the Verdun front thundered, and Clemenceau was at his fiercest in public broils, that Claude Monet at last completed the erection of a studio in which he could carry out these gigantic canvases.

To Giverny, to Claude Monet and his garden, Clemenceau used to drive down of a Sunday, leaving the war behind him, and watch the work progressing.

CLAUDE MONET *and* HIS GARDEN

To Giverny he was summoned when appalling disaster fell on the peaceful labourer; and after total blindness was averted, to Giverny Clemenceau must come and watch Monet attacking again those problems which his marvellous vision had surmounted, but which now must be faced with a deranged and one-sided machinery of sight.

The end of that struggle, the fruits of victory, are to be seen there in the Orangerie; yet for me those pictures will never separate themselves from the place of their creation. When I saw Monet's garden first, on a glorious summer day of 1932, I thought I had never met so rare and significant a beauty. Now that I know the story, the garden means more; it is the scene of a great man's final triumph, first over the hostilities of a criticism which could not believe that in art there could have been found a new way, and then over that last stab of fate which struck at the very organ through which alone triumph was possible.

Yet if that were all it meant to me, I do not think I should attempt this writing; the concern would be too strictly with the artist's work, and the heresy hunt launched against him. It is because the whole setting —that countryside of land richly cultivated beside the shining waterway, busy but noiseless, from Paris to the sea; the woods on the slopes above it, tended like all timber in a land where nothing goes to waste; the quiet village which Monet's residence has glorified, drawing to it other artists, content, as he was, to beautify by modest touches, adorning yet leaving the essential unchanged; the simple farm-house where he lived, whose only luxury is the garden that once was ragged orchard and a fringe of swamp; the vision of the old painter with his Olympian beard and big straw hat pottering among the flowers when he left his easel, or deep in meditation on a seat by the water's edge, as he watched the lilies poise over the clouds reflected in that mirror; finally, the old statesman coming down there with a mind equipped, alert and furnished to respond to every imaginable stimulus—all this taken together, this mixture of rustic simplicity with the highest intellectual energy and the last refinements of culture—all these, in their synthesis (as the modern phrase goes) are to me France.

The story of which I try to sketch some aspects would, if it were fitly recounted, be the story of an artistic movement in which by general admission France has given the lead to Europe and in which Monet was really the leader of France. French writers have dealt with it on this side of intellectual mastery. My concern, writing for an English-speaking public, is rather with the scene and the setting, for these, at least to a foreigner, are not less significant.

Monet is not one of the painters whose work is associated definitely with one particular region; he painted in many lands or, to put it more truly, by many waters; on the coasts of the Adriatic, of the Channel, of the Atlantic, of the Mediterranean. Yet by birth and upbringing, and most decisively by his choice of a home, he belongs to the Seine from Paris to the sea; and just as the Thames from Oxford down is not indeed all England, but quintessential England, so is the lower Seine quintessential France. Monet was born in Paris; he grew up in Havre, where the Seine enters the sea, and there found his vocation; he went back to Paris for his training, and for much of his early work he chose his subjects at places like Argenteuil, or Asnières, only just outside the capital. In middle life, when he could fix an abiding place, he chose it at Giverny, halfway between Paris and Rouen; and though much by which he is best known was done in long excursions away from this base, yet he is to all time the Master of Giverny.

What I write of is in the main concerned with his relation to Giverny. Still, in the first place, the early stages of his life have to be sketched.

CHAPTER II

EARLY LIFE AND ASSOCIATION
WITH BOUDIN

Monet's was an immensely long life; eighty-six years of it. Painters last longer than other men; theirs is a health-giving occupation; much of it (often at least) spent in the open air, all of it spent in work which is of the hand as well as of the brain; needing those continual small dexterities that are in themselves a physical delight, and exercise the body, though they do not strain it like the labourer's or the athlete's. Titian and Turner went on as long as Monet. But I do not think that in any other case the creative impulse prolonged itself with such fire, seeking always an expression less material, more etherealised, more lyrical. Monet was, as Clemenceau says, a lyrical artist, and never so lyrical as when he painted the *nymphœas* which are in the Orangerie.

This long span of life falls into halves, of forty-three years, and the marking point is 1883, when he was able to make his home at Giverny. Until then, he seldom had a settled dwelling-place; one may say that he had hardly the means to live. The pursuit of his art seemed to have sentenced him to perpetual poverty.

Yet hardship was not what he was born to. His parents, who came from Lyons, were established at Paris in the Rue Laffitte as grocers; not successful, but not needy; when the shopkeeping in Paris failed, they went down to join relations in Havre, Monsieur and Madame Lecadre, who were in a big way of the same business. Claude Monet grew up in the seaport where the Seine enters the sea, in sight of blue water and among the ships which provisioned themselves at his uncle's shop.

He was only five when this change in his surroundings happened; a robustious healthy black-haired truant of a boy who slipped away from school whenever he could, to run about the cliffs or go paddling on the beach. The only thing he wanted to do indoors was to draw, and although his father and mother, and indeed the whole circle in which he lived, had a contempt for the arts in general, his aunt, Madame Lecadre, painted genteelly in watercolours and hung her room with a few pictures. But her nephew's artistic achievements of this time were not genteel; he had so much talent for caricatures, and exercised it so freely, that by the time he was fifteen, a frame-maker at Havre (the only shop in the town that dealt in art products) was buying these sketches and exhibiting them in his window. People came to young Monet offering him ten francs, twenty francs, to draw a sketch of them. This went on admirably, and the talented youth could fix on twenty francs as his standard charge; what is more, he could do seven or eight of the sketches in the day. 'If I'd gone on,' he said later, 'I should be a millionaire to-day.'

Meantime, however, the frame-maker was exhibiting in the same window little sea pieces by an artist called Boudin; and young Monet did not like them. They were not executed at all in accordance with the prevailing ideas of what a picture should be, with light and shade properly grouped and contrasted. But this Boudin was the son of a seaman, skipper of a boat carrying goods between Rouen and Honfleur; at least he knew how to rig a boat. He also had been scribbling with a pencil from childhood; had been apprenticed to a printer, and had started a stationery shop in Honfleur. Well-known artists, coming down to work on the Norman coasts, came in to buy pencils or sketching-blocks; they saw the shopkeeper's sketches, showed him their own work, and, in short, fired him with the desire to be a painter too. Troyon especially, then a most successful artist, encouraged him and prompted some wealthy people in Havre to provide him with fifty pounds a year for three years study in Paris. But Boudin was back in a few months, unable to endure the city life; out on his cliffs, watching the boats sailing by, he tried to fix exactly what he saw, having become aware that the painters in fashion (except Corot at times) either did not see or did not attempt to reproduce what he saw in the shifting colour of the universe. He wanted to achieve painting that should have daylight in it, not the light of a studio. And so this candid enthusiast, who could not see the sky without a torturing desire to reproduce its splendour, not only followed his own guiding impulse, but, like other enthusiasts, wanted to make disciples. One day in the frame-maker's shop, painter and caricaturist met. 'So, young man,' said Boudin, 'it's you who do these little things. They have something in them—why not try painting?' The young man who could sell as many sketches as he liked, and probably was well aware that the painter could not sell any, listened with a kind of pitying condescension, but finally agreed to go out for a day's work in the open air. And then he saw Boudin painting a grey cloud; building up the body of it with subtle gradations, pinks and mauves fusing, until there really was a cloud there. 'Then' (Claude Monet said long after) 'it was like a veil tearing. I understood; I knew what painting might be.'

They worked together for several months, Boudin preaching to him that work done in the studio would never have the life and force of what is painted face to face with nature. In 1856, when Boudin showed a little group of seascapes at Rouen, there was a view of Rouelles by Claude Monet shown along with them, which the local press described as 'sharing the qualities of M. Boudin's work'.

But the younger man soon felt the need for other contacts. Boudin was a painter, not a master; in the room of his aunt Lecadre he had found a canvas which seemed to give him an idea of what modern painting by a master might be; it was signed 'Daubigny'. Only at Paris he could hope to see the work of modern masters, and he begged his father to let him go to Paris and study. M. Monet asked the municipality of Havre for a scholarship, and all the town councillors were well aware of the son's gifts as a draughtsman; but the sample of painting which he submitted did not please them at all, and in May 1859 they refused the application, suggesting that the young man should apply himself to something more 'serious' than an art. However, by that time, the young man had drawn out the money accumulated from his caricatures—two thousand francs of it—and set off for Paris, where Boudin gave him an introduction to Troyon.

That famous man was not discouraging about the studies of still life which the beginner showed him; he recognised a sense of colour. 'But,' he said, 'this comes too easy to you; go to an academy and learn to draw the figure. Concentrate on draughtsmanship, but now and then take a run into the country; make sketches, carry them as far as you can. Go to the Louvre and copy; and come and show me what you are doing.' It was the traditional advice, given friendlily; and it sent young Monet to the academy of one

Suisse. Here he made his first alliance among those who with him were to become first hooted and then illustrious under the name of Impressionists. He met Camille Pissarro, who for a couple of years had been working in this school. Pissarro had been privileged to meet Corot; had received encouragement and good advice from one who was a recognised master. By this time—it was 1859—the Barbizon school had fought and won their battle against the upholders of a tradition in which a picture was to be in the main a way of telling a story, through line and colour combined according to recognised rules. Monet was unstinted in admiration for Corot; but he never lost his attachment to the painter whose excellence he had discovered for himself in his Aunt Lecadre's drawing-room. The little Daubigny had been brought with him to Paris, and when he found how its painter was reputed he was proud of this certificate for the discernment of his eye.

However, the certificate did not remain long in his possession. Art students are the same in all generations; only their haunts change. At this moment they affected the Brasserie des Martyrs, and Monet was among the regular frequenters of this establishment, where the young pointed out to each other personages of growing repute, such as Baudelaire, Alphonse Daudet, Theodore de Banville and the Anglo-Belgian painter, Alfred Stevens. They fought over their pre-

ferences among the reigning masters; Ingres had his
votaries of course; others were for Delacroix; others
for Puvis de Chavannes. Monet, never a great talker,
sat and listened, and sketched the types he saw. But he
was a lusty young man; the portrait of him at eighteen
by Déodat de Sévérac, prefixed to M. Geffroy's volume, shows heavy shoulders, massive arms resting on
the back of a chair, a crop of black hair combed back
from a strongly modelled forehead and falling down
in abundance to the neck; not the kind of young man
who would stay behind when his comrades wanted to
go gallivanting. One day, however, he was short of
money; they were all short of money; then an idea
struck Monet. There was his Daubigny—the charming
little vintage scene. Into a cab they got and the
Daubigny with them, off to the picture dealers; but
nobody would buy it till at last in the Rue de Bac one
named Thomas ('I shall never forget him,' Monet
said, when he recalled this adventure), offered sixteen
pounds—but only on condition that Daubigny himself certified the picture to be genuine. Nobody knew
the painter; Monet was too shy to intrude on him;
but one of the others had more courage; they went to
Daubigny's studio and the great man was friendly.
He gave the signature they wanted and they got the
four hundred francs.

Later in life, Monet was of opinion that the
Brasserie des Martyrs and all that side of student life

had been doing him harm, as no doubt it has done to many. At all events, a break in his existence put an end to it. Conscription was then not universal, names were drawn by ballot; and he was among the unlucky. Under other circumstances his well-to-do relations would have bought a substitute, as was the usage; but they thought he was doing no good at Paris, they had no tenderness for his vocation, and left him to be shipped off to Algiers in the Chasseurs d'Afrique.

He had no bad word to say of this experience; he thought it steadied him, and ended tendencies towards too many brasseries. Moreover, the brilliant sunshine was a revelation, and he contrived to get furloughs by painting a portrait of his captain. But the climate told on his health, and after a year and a half he was sent home to France on six months' sick-leave. Back in Havre, he fell to work with his palette more passionately than ever; and on the cliffs by the town a chance acquaintance told him that Jongkind, one of the younger men whose work he had seen and admired in Paris, was now at Honfleur and could be met. So began a new alliance that fortified his attachment to work in the open air.

Before the sick-leave was ended, his relations, seeing that nothing could shake his vocation, bought him out of the army and provided him with means to return to Paris. He was back there by the spring of 1862.

A few months later Clemenceau, a medical student,

The Church and Graveyard at Giverny

was sent to jail by the government of the Second Empire for revolutionary republican propaganda. His father, a doctor at Nantes, had had the same experience four years earlier.

We cannot be certain when Monet and Clemenceau first met; but it was in the Quartier Latin, where one was walking the hospitals and the other working at a studio. Possibly it was before 1860, when Monet was sent to Africa; possibly after his return in 1862, and before 1865, when the young doctor emigrated to America. The brasseries and cafés of Montparnasse were then as they are still, a common playground to all the student tribe. Moreover, they had two friends in common who brought them together—a young doctor from Nantes, and a politician, also from the South-West. Both these men had already early sea pieces by Monet—gifts from the artist. There is no suggestion in what Clemenceau tells that he and Monet were intimates in these days. Intimacy came much later, when both in their very different ways had been in many battles, and had won fame. One thing, however, is sure; early or late, politics were not the bond of union. Monet was a revolutionary and a rebel in his art, but outside it he concerned himself with little. On the other hand, art, letters, everything interested Georges Clemenceau.

CHAPTER III

EXHIBITING AT THE SALON

T HE rebel in Claude Monet was very soon evident after he had come back, in Paris, and set to work in good earnest; for Africa, as he said, had put ballast in his head, and there was no more gallivanting, but a grim struggle to find his feet in the assured vocation. His family had sent him up with an introduction to a personage with whom the Lecadres were connected by marriage—Toulmouche, a successful painter of popular anecdotes. Toulmouche recommended the young man to pursue his studies under Gleyre, who was indeed, as Monet has testified, a serious and conscientious worker, but in a style that was no use at all to his new pupil. Monet working from the nude model painted what he saw; and Gleyre admitted that it was good work—but too like nature. The shoulders were too heavy, the feet too big. Art, he said, should idealise; Praxiteles made a perfection generalised from the beauty of a hundred forms, suppressing all that fell short of perfection. The artist should always think of the antique. 'But,' said Monet, 'I can only paint what I see;' and other students, like-minded with him, took counsel together. For, just as he had met

19

Pissarro at the Académie Suisse, here in Gleyre's studio he fell in with real talents. Renoir was one, Sisley another; a third was Bazille, who did not live to see the fight won. 'Let's get out of here,' said Monet, 'it isn't good for the health, there isn't enough sincerity.' So after a fortnight of it, they said goodbye to Gleyre and followed their own devices. Monet was soon back by the sea, at Honfleur, along with Boudin and Jongkind, working passionately in the open air. By 1865 he had advanced far enough to send to the Salon two studies of the Norman Coast which were accepted. Two critics of the exhibition had the discernment to pick out these works by an unknown hand, recognising a boldness and originality in his way of seeing nature; and they predicted a notable future for this painter of the sea. Neither called him a revolutionary; but one, Paul Martz, noted the lack of *finesse* in his work.

Looking back on it, one seems to see that the defects of Monet's qualities must have stood specially in the way with the French public, which is always in love with delicate ingenuity, dainty precision of touch and clean finish. These are the superficial qualities of the French genius, whether in literature or art. A hundred Frenchmen have shown, in all the arts, the rude force, the powerful modelling, the strength drawn from the land, deeply characteristic of a country where roots are more deeply planted in the soil than anywhere else in Europe; but none of these has succeeded in France without a struggle, and none found it rougher than Claude Monet. Whatever he did, first to last, had weight and had force; but first and last it was done with a heavy hand; and since what allured him first and last to represent was the impalpable, the vibrant atmosphere in which things have their being, it is little wonder if the way was hard. He never made it easy for himself. Even in France (though not so slavishly as in England), an artist is expected by critics and the public to keep well within the lines of his original endeavour. Monet had begun with sea pieces. Next year he was off completely on another bent; and the new attempt was in two ways revolutionary—by its subject and by its treatment of the subject. It represented a picnic party in a glade at Fontainebleau.

The generation of Monet's forerunners, and most notably Jean François Millet, had succeeded in establishing that the peasant in peasant dress offers a proper theme for painting. Apart from this, uniforms, state robes or costumes consecrated by the art of earlier centuries, were obligatory—with a preference for the antique. To paint people wearing mackintoshes, bowler hats or the like was a bold innovation; but it had been attempted by one painter in especial, Edouard Manet. He also had done a *Déjeuner sur l'herbe*; and was no way pleased to learn that his theme was being taken up again by another artist, of a name so inconveniently similar.

This was indeed only a small part of the similarity; for Monet at this period, when he painted figures, saw them through eyes affected by Manet's vision. There was a likeness of temperament. Both men insisted on seeing people exactly as they were; in both there was an insistence on the characteristic outline of each personage which need only be pushed a little further to become caricature. Indeed in the Tate Gallery at London there is a picture by Manet of Madame Manet with a cat on her ample lap, and a picture by Monet of a lady reclining, a shapeless bundle on a sunlit bench, and it would be hard to decide which of the two shows less consideration for the sitter's vanity. But that was what they saw, and they put it down; so long as the light caressed the rotundities, they asked no more.

But in Monet's *Déjeuner sur l'herbe* there was already present an attempt not found in the elder man's work; for Manet was still painting in a discreetly managed and filtered studio light. Monet went at his huge canvas in the open and flooded all with sunlight streaming in through the trees. The figures were secondary to the lights, not the illumination to the figures. 'The light is the real person in a picture,' he said, long after. For him this was always true, when

Camille in Monet's Garden at Argenteuil

Painted in 1875

he was unknown, or was made only notorious by ridicule, just as when he was famous. A great painter came to look at this effort, curious about a young man who was 'painting something else than angels'. This was Gustave Courbet, and Monet since first he came to Paris as a boy had been expressing reverence for Courbet's work. The master had criticisms to offer; Monet tried to alter his work, was discontented with the result, and decided to try something else. Within four days he produced his study of a lady in green silk dress, displayed as she walks away; the head, just turned, gives us a likeness that is of interest in the story; for Camille, *la Dame à la robe verte*, became Monet's wife and the mother of his children. So early as this, the young artist had other lives than his own to fend for.

Camille was accepted for the Salon of 1866; it was bought for thirty pounds by a well-known man of letters, Arsène Houssaye. It was praised enthusiastically by Emile Zolà, then fighting the battle of realism in art as well as in fiction. Monet, he said, was unknown to him but now seemed to be an old friend; a live man in a crowd of eunuchs.

Friendship followed naturally; and to know Zolà was to know the painter whom above all he was concerned to champion, Paul Cézanne, soon a member of the militant revolutionary group in paint.

Manet was in a sense their acknowledged leader; he had a position in society, and a clever tongue to champion the cause of an art which sought for new advances, not mere repetition. But the others were fighting for dear life, and none of them harder put to it than Monet. The success of his *Camille* was his last lucky hit in the Salon. Next year a huge canvas by him was refused, *Femmes au Jardin.* It was painted at Ville d'Avray, where he had fled to escape the importunity of creditors (in these early years his property was seized several times), and in order to carry out his work in the open air he dug a deep trench in the garden and arranged a frame with ropes and pulleys so that the canvas could travel up and down to be within his reach.

The picture is in the Louvre now, more than half a century after the hanging committee refused it for the Salon. Four women (or rather several versions of the same woman; models cost money and Camille clearly posed for two or three of the figures) are standing or sitting in a garden among shrubs and flowers; the huge crinolines make a light-coloured pattern which shows already a superb decorative sense. But what interests me here is to note that wherever Monet established himself, there had to be a garden. His pictures prove it; there is one at Argenteuil on the outskirts of Paris, painted early in the 'seventies; another, a year or two later, at Véthueil further down the Seine —where he paused for some years on the way, as it were, to his final resting-place at Giverny.

Yet before these days, after the rejection of his big canvas, he had gone back to his own country and worked there again along with Boudin and Jongkind, sending up pictures of boats in harbour to the Salons of 1868 and 1869. Courbet had joined the group and inevitably influenced the younger men; yet he in return was affected by their refusal not merely to accept studio lighting, the picture lit as if by a hole in the top of a cave. Nor were they content, as Corot and Millet had been, to choose effects of twilight or grey skies. They wanted full sunlight, light everywhere, *la peinture claire*.

A couple of pictures in the Tate Gallery enable us to get some notion of Monet's work at this period; for they are hung, as they should be, near others by Boudin. Both of Monet's are seaside studies; it should be realised that for the first ten years of Monet's career people thought of him mostly as a painter of seascapes. But in both the background of sea is secondary to an attempt to paint figures in the open air. In other words, we find the young painter occupied chiefly with the technical problem, and much more under another man's influence than ever again. He is seeing figures as Manet would have seen them, but seeing with his own eyes the impact of actual light. He is trying to do what did not interest him when he came fully to himself; for then figures disappeared altogether from his compositions. Boudin, on the other hand, as seen in the Tate, has thoroughly found his way, grouping his figures admirably for the design, yet always concentrated on the beauty of sea and sky to which the figure group is quite secondary.

Jongkind is represented in the same room, but it is in the Camondo Collection at the Louvre that one realises the close affinity, and so to say comradeship, between the work of this engaging Dutchman and that of Boudin. The same seas are observed through eyes akin to each other; though oddly enough the Dutchman seems to have more gaiety and brilliance. Monet when he came to full possession of his powers showed us sea pictures, in a sense no truer, yet with a tidal swing in them that neither Boudin nor Jongkind ever reached to.

The three of them working together knew good companionship. But these were years of distress and debt for all the young group. The Salon of 1870 refused what Monet sent in; and then came an upheaval for the whole of France. War was declared on Prussia. There was not then universal conscription. One of the group, Bazille, volunteered and was killed in an early skirmish; Monet, like Pissarro, crossed the Channel, and sought what could be found in London.

At the same time Clemenceau, married and settled in America after the only period of tranquillity in his life, was hurrying back to play his part in the struggle, and to see the Republic proclaimed.

It is natural enough that in his life of Monet, Clemenceau makes no mention of Monet's attitude in this crisis. So great a divergence in the conception of duty might well have broken friendship. Yet the Tiger always loved a fighting man who fought for principles that he believed in; he knew that there were more ways than one of being a combatant; and one thing he makes plain from the first page to the last: Claude Monet's life is a long record of indomitable courage in the unswerving pursuit of an ideal.

CHAPTER IV

DURAND RUEL AND HARD TIMES

M ONET'S STAY in London brought him no help
from England. A letter from Pissarro who had
joined him says that the English painters were not
friendly; that the world of art was entirely commer-
cial. But they saw and studied Turner's work, and
though accounts of the effect that it produced on the
Frenchmen vary, it is easier to believe those who say
that Monet recognised a great visionary: one who was
what Clemenceau called Monet, a lyrical poet in paint.
Paul Signac, one of the Neo-Impressionist school who
sought to reduce to a formula Monet's practice of
breaking up light into its components, says also definitely that Turner's treatment of snow was a revelation.
What they had sought and failed to obtain by large
dashes of silver white, Turner secured by a quantity of
touches of varying colour side by side, which at the
proper distance gave the brilliancy of a snow-white
scene.

A glance at Monet's study in the Tate Gallery of
some houses at Véthueil under snow, with the ice-
choked river in front of them, will confirm this. It

has the sparkle of a winter scene; but there is far more blue paint than white on the canvas; and little touches of pink here and there throw the white into relief.

As to Monet's general attitude to Turner, one thing should be noted. Of all the work of French masters at the Louvre, his choice was for Watteau's *Embarquement pour Cythère*. No other picture in the Louvre is so like a Turner—though for that matter none is less like a Claude Monet. But it is inconceivable that one who admired so much that earlier masterpiece should not have had admiration for the Englishman's work, so like it, less by imitation than by a kinship of imagination.

Though England was in no way kind to these penniless artists, it was in London that they met the man who was to be most decisively their backer and that of all their school. This was the famous picture dealer, Durand Ruel. His father, whose business he inherited, had shown his discernment from 1830 onwards by buying the work of Delacroix, Corot and Millet and the rest when they were almost as completely neglected or decried as Monet's group came to be in the 'seventies. The son, who was now reaping the fruits of his father's discernment in money and prestige, chanced to be in England on his own business. So also was that great artist Daubigny, on whom ten years earlier young Monet and his companions had descended

Monet's Seat

with the urgent entreaty that he should enable them to cash a picture. Doubtless the acquaintance had developed; at all events the established master had watched the progress of his admirer, and coming upon Monet forlorn in this strange capital, he took him by the hand and brought him to Durand Ruel, saying, 'Here is a young man who will be better than any of us (*plus fort que nous tous*)'. When the dealer hesitated—and, as the next ten years proved, had cause to hesitate—Daubigny clinched the matter by saying: 'If you take his work and cannot dispose of it, you shall have works of mine (since you like them) in exchange.' So Durand Ruel bought from Monet, who brought Pissarro to him, and from him also the dealer acquired a couple of small canvases. Later, when they were back in Paris, they brought Renoir to this friendly door; for the group held solidly together, and in the last resort their few francs were always at each other's service. But Daubigny's generosity was of another kind, for he stood in no need of help; and this is a pleasant thing to remember in front of one of his serene and beautiful landscapes. Still, artists then had need to stand together; the society of that time in Paris allowed them no contacts. They were *cabotins* and vagrants, as much as the actors.

It was many a long year yet before Durand Ruel's new investments could justify themselves, and for many a long year canvases of the group accumulated with him. Manifestly he could not do more than help to tide them over. Just to live by, every penny was needed, and every penny was not enough.

In 1872 Monet came back to France; he had made some stay in Holland and painted there also, canals, barges, and windmills, solid, sober work; something of the deadness of those waters gets into these pictures; but they were admired. Daubigny, in addition to his other friendly offices, bought one of them. On his death in 1878, Duret, a critic of discernment, went to the sale of the painter's effects, hoping to acquire the Monet, but could see no trace of it. A few days later he chanced in an auction to see a confused mass—the remnants of Daubigny's property, not considered worth inventory. They were auctioned; he got the Monet for 80 francs: years later he sold it for 5000 to Durand Ruel, who later still got 30,000 for it.

One may judge from this how things were in 1872 when Monet established himself on the bank of a river that had more life in it than the Dutch canals. At Argenteuil Paris was only a few miles off, and he could get up to the Avenue de Clichy for weekly assemblies of the Group in the Café Guerbois. It may have been at Argenteuil that he and Renoir got hold of a plot of ground, dug it (look at the two men's work and you will be sure that Monet did most of the digging), planted it with potatoes and lived on the results for the best part of a year. Monet was not of peasant stock, but the peasant type of France comes out in him all through—the French tiller of the soil who by some special dispensation so easily acquires the most refined cultivation, yet can pass on to his descendants something rough and primitive, in close sympathy with the fertile earth.

There was a garden at Argenteuil too; he has painted Camille in it; and Renoir painted the artist there, bearded now, pipe in mouth, and for a symbol of his passion, a watering-pot in his hand. But there was another side to the life at Argenteuil; he had got a floating work-room, a sort of small houseboat, with a little cabin aft; and Manet painted him and Camille afloat on it, she at some stitchery, he with his palette trying for the hundredth time to catch the splashing of sunlight on the flowing water and the transparencies that his eye divined. Manet called the picture *Monet's Studio*. Monet himself would never admit that he had a studio at all. Drawing could be done indoors, but painting for him was only to be accomplished in the open air.

It began to be clear now what the new school was after—though as yet only certain persons recognised that they were after something intelligible and not merely daubing on paint as a child might do—which is what the less instructed critics said of them. Working as they did, light and air assumed a new importance: for Claude Monet indeed, they were increasingly the first consideration. In the studio one could produce a constant and more or less uniform illumination, divisible into light and shade; in the open, nothing was constant, and when the sun shone there was brilliance everywhere. Shadows varied in colour no less than lights; what was more, under a full sun, colour was absorbed. All this group, but Monet most of all, set out to paint the world as they saw it and not as it had been transposed and interpreted under studio conditions. Monet's distinguishing equipment was an extraordinary power of vision. Cézanne once said of him, 'The man is nothing but an eye: but what an eye!' There was indeed a great deal more than an eye there; there was a lyrical poet; but first of all in the artist's evolution, Monet's eye had to determine what it really could see when it looked hard at light or at shadow. All those who write of the man from personal knowledge dwell on the piercing quality of his glance; Clemenceau describes it as driving into the object like bullets. However one describes it, this vision distinguished what the ordinary man could not perceive—shadow, even when it seemed most uniform, lit up by little sparks of colour, chiefly orange and violet; and to obtain the living quality of what he represented, he flecked his canvas with their brilliance, recognising that at the proper distance they would not be seen as flecks but would merge, as in nature, into one tone.

At the very same time, men of science were busy, de-composing light into the different radiations which are fused in the lens of the eye—a new discovery in knowledge. Of this Monet knew nothing; only his eye guided him; but his unaided vision was finding out for itself what laboratory experiment with complex machinery determined and taught the world. After the work of Monet and his group—but chiefly of Monet —painting could no more be precisely what it was before, than could science after the spectroscope had been discovered.

CHAPTER V

THE PUBLIC AND IMPRESSIONISM

IT IS a commonplace that in each generation some new interpretation of the world is presented and finds a public unaccustomed to it and therefore hostile; yet gradually the strange grows familiar, easy to assimilate and enjoy. But in the case of Monet and his group the novelty was more startling, because it involved a change even in the physical approach. The public knew in a general way that a picture should be seen from an appropriate distance; none the less it inclined to admire the artist whose execution could be best appreciated under a microscope. At this very time Meissonier was painting studies of horses whose every hair almost seemed traceable. With Monet, the nearer you approached, the less you saw; even at the utmost of arms-length, the picture was apt to be confused; and it seemed incredible that a man in the act of painting should not see the canvas as it was meant to be seen. Yet, for instance, in the Tate Gallery, there is a picture of Rouen Cathedral which even from a couple of yards away looks like a rubble of brick-dust, glued on. Cross the room, and you see emerging from white and rosy mists the vast front with all the complexity of its ornament incomparably suggested, though nothing is given in detail.

This is not a normal example of Monet's painting, and it is open to many objections. Renoir, who experimented with this particular method, gave it up and said he liked a canvas to tempt his hand to caress it; some of these pictures made him want to strike a match on them. There is very little of the sensuous strokable quality in Monet's work; there is a great deal of it in Renoir's. Monet, especially in his early period, preferred to leave his touches distinct on the canvas; to fix and unite them would probably have seemed to him a sacrifice of the vibrant brilliance that he sought to reproduce. On the other hand Renoir was just as disposed as Monet to emphasise the blueness in shadows among leafage, or lilac in tree shadows on the ground; and the Salon would have none of him—would have none of them. So, at Monet's instigation, they decided to hold an exhibition of their own. It ran from mid-April to mid-May in 1874 in Nadar's gallery on the Boulevard des Capucines. Manet stood out of it; but his sister-in-law, Berthe Morisot, a delightful artist, the charm of whose work can be best appreciated in the Camondo Collection at the Louvre (but the Tate has examples of it), was there. Boudin also was there, who had by this time reached some modest prosperity, still painting the light of day with grace

Monet's Garden at Argenteuil
Painted in 1873

and with sincerity, but using a technique to which critics and public were accustomed. A more famous artist, Degas, was there too, whose originality, though not less, was different from that of the Impressionists —as they now began to be called. For among Monet's landscapes was one called *Impression: Soleil levant*: an indication of fishing-boats faintly seen through mists at dawn. One of the smart journalists who abound even more in Paris than elsewhere pitched upon Monet's title to echo in his article for the *Charivari* the general tone of derision which he found prevailing among those who visited the show. 'Impression; the very thing: certainly I was *impressionné*. How bold! how easy! a piece of daubed paper would be even more impressionist than this seascape.' And so the name was taken up, and the group themselves definitely accepted it. Very well, they would be impressionists.

Hardly anyone had a good word to say of them, and next spring when Durand Ruel organised a sale of pictures by Monet, Renoir, Sisley and Berthe Morisot, there was actually a hostile demonstration: police had to be brought in to prevent people from sticking their umbrellas through the canvases. None of the pictures fetched so much as twenty pounds, many sold for the price of the frames. Twenty years later they would have been cheap at twenty times as much; but there is an Irish saying, 'Live, horse, and you will get grass', and it is not a consoling one. Things were no better in 1876 when a new exhibition was held, Manet this time exhibiting with the others. Jules Claretie, a man of wit and intelligence, director of the *Comédie Française*, complained that this new school of landscape seemed to have declared war on beauty. Manet, he said, had represented the Seine by a crude patch of blue; and Manet seemed modest and timid beside Monet. What would be the end of it with artists who tried to banish shadow and darkness from the world altogether?

Another critic, less polite, said that there was a danger lest pictures of this kind should set the bus-horses bolting; and another, that the place for the artists was in a lunatic asylum. But a writer of real note, Castagnary, recognised the value of a movement which was going to rid landscape painting for ever of bitumen.

Meantime, the group hung together. There is a letter from Manet in 1875 to a friendly man of letters, Duret, saying that he had found Monet terribly downcast and in difficulties, and proposing that the two of them should combine to offer, through some third person, a thousand francs (forty pounds) for ten of his canvases.

There are some heartrending extracts from Monet's letters (given by Madame de Fels) to one of the few who were buying his works. At this time, he had

Vétheuil under Snow

Painted in 1881

moved from the neighbourhood of Paris—but not from its river—to Véthueil, a beautiful village on the left bank of the winding stretch between Mantes and Vernon; rising steeply on the side of a *coteau*, with a superb old church dominating the whole. Here he painted interminably; for scores of studies of it survive, though already it was his custom when a canvas displeased to slash it across with a penknife, as if he was disembowelling an enemy. Winter and summer he painted here, for half the pictures are scenes of snow, or of ice breaking up on the river; neither snow nor rain would keep this worker indoors. But when his wife and child were ill, and there was no one but himself to attend to them, work had to stop, and expenses would not. So he writes to a purchaser who has already advanced him money for certain canvases, making excuse for his delay, and saying that Caillebotte, another painter and a friend, had preserved one of the slashed-open canvases; it might be put together, and if so he would be only in debt for one more.

The answer to this was unfriendly and came in an evil hour. Camille died, leaving him with a delicate child on his hands, and creditors threatening to seize his few sticks of furniture, while he hunted from door to door for the loan of another couple of pounds. For all the resolution of his temper, he was a moody man, and in these days his despair was black, and he had lost hope of ever finding appreciation. There is a letter from Caillebotte, a good friend, comparatively a rich man, a painter of pictures as well as a buyer of them who tried to reason him out of his discouragement and implored him to send up as many works as possible for that year's exhibition of the group.

But when two canvases made their appearance, both had been slashed across; they had been sent in sheer despair. Yet Caillebotte wrote that one of them was going to be bought by an American lady, Miss Cassatt, who figured among the group of Impressionist painters. Monet had good reason before long to be thankful to America, where he found a market sooner than in France. Miss Cassatt has the honour to figure in that gathering of works by foreign painters which the French Government has detached from the main collection at the Luxembourg, and housed together at the Jeu de Paume—a building which makes a pendant to the Orangerie at the west end of the Tuileries.

As to Caillebotte, all picture lovers are his debtors. He could give, and did give, the practical aid of buying work from these struggling people. But to be bought by such a judge was a true encouragement. In the Collection which he bequeathed at his death to the Luxembourg—it is now in the Louvre—there is one canvas by himself, a study of two workmen planing smooth a floor, perfectly admirable both in drawing and composition. Much of Monet's work is in the collection, yet not the best of it; the defect of Caille-

Monet's Garden at Véthueil
   Painted in 1881

botte's choice is that it was made partly from the desire to give assistance. I do not think that anyone should be the less grateful to his memory.

He had, however, another link with Monet in later and more prosperous days, for he also was a passionate gardener. It may be that the flowers which Monet has shown adorning his garden at Argenteuil came as a friendly gift from this rich neighbour; for that was where they first grew acquainted. But certainly when Monet's garden at Giverny was in the making, Caillebotte was a chief counsellor in the choosing and laying out.

CHAPTER VI

HARD TIMES

DURING THESE years in the latter half of the 'eighties while Monet was living in a cabin at Véthueil with misery about him, and selling his pictures (when he could) for an average of four pounds a canvas, the Impressionist movement defined itself and gained a beginning of recognition. He himself also altered his course, or limited it; there are no more studies of figures in the open air; nothing but pure landscape. In this as in all else he acted not on theory but on a profound impulse. Geffroy quotes a saying of his: 'I paint as a bird sings.' But Geffroy and the rest have helped us to define what the song was about.

Great landscape painters—Turner is a superb example—had built up imaginary landscapes, based it is true on a profound knowledge of living forms, yet still put together after architectural conventions, and illuminated by a light skilfully and deliberately arranged. Monet on the other hand persisted in his affirmation that he had made in Gleyre's studio: 'I can paint only what I see.' The first concern for him was to choose among the endless combinations of the world presented to his vision what could make a picture;

for no artist ever had more strongly the sense of a pattern. A famous canvas of these years representing a group of white turkeys illustrates this quality in its most obvious form; but indeed the final example is in the living picture that he made at Giverny and in his paintings from it. Water-lilies in his pond were set group by group into a larger grouping, apparently accidental, having no stiff symmetry, yet planned and spaced in an order which ceaseless care from that day to this was to maintain.

Yet form was not his inspiration. Coloured shapes gave only the framework, the metre and the rhythm of his poem. The song was about light; even when he painted a water-lily group of flowers and flat leaves—and what else in nature is so sculpturesque?—his concern was less with the form than the vibrant atmosphere it bathed in. He painted the world he saw; but the world of sense perception is one of unstable images, perpetually altered by the fleeting incidence of light and shade. It is altered far more rapidly and far more manifestly under a sky where clouds chase each other, when from day to day and hour to hour the moisture in the atmosphere varies and in varying alters the quality of the liquid air through which forms are revealed. Monet was a Frenchman of the North; of the Atlantic and the Channel, not of the Mediterranean; change of effect was what he naturally looked for. A German writer on *The Spirit of France* has said recently that Im-

The Full Length of the Pond

pressionism could only have originated among the mingled mists and sunshine, the quivering light and shade, which are special to the valley of the Seine. It was natural that Cézanne, come like his friend and champion Zolà from Aix in the hard sunlight of Provence, should bring out beyond others in his work the palpable solidity of forms; and natural that Monet formed in the lower Seine valley should be for ever in pursuit of the impalpable, the flickering movements that chase each other over the face of things. This is not to say that his work lacks mass and weight: the man himself was too powerful, too solid for that. When the cathedral of Rouen emerges through the luminous mist, it is a great rock emerging; when he paints the flank of the Seine's *coteau* opposite Giverny (there is a picture of it in the Rouen Gallery), it is a mountain slope breathing. Yet always it is the light that gives life. At Rouen again, there is another study of the cathedral's south doorway, seen in a grey light; a cold picture, yet what it makes one feel is the efflorescence, the living skin that comes on old buildings, created through centuries by the enveloping air and revealed to such eyes as Monet's by the transitory incidence of that very light, which makes the stone germinate and blossom.

He hated darkness; every room, everywhere that he lived, must be as far as possible open to the light; for he felt and thought, he existed, through his eyes. If to

Sometimes they wanted to help us. But they were not gambling on our chances.'

Another buyer was Faure, a singer at the Opera, who had the courage to face public derision in the papers for his odd taste in buying; but once at least he lacked discernment. Monet came in from Véthueil with a study of early light, forms faintly indicated, a subtle suggestion of dawn just tinging the old town and its church into life. The price he asked was fifty francs—what this purchaser habitually paid. Faure looked at it and said: 'Go back and put some painting in: there is nothing there. I don't buy blank canvases.' Years passed, Monet was selling his pictures now; Faure came to his studio and looking round caught sight of this delicate impression, and said, 'I must have that: what do you want, six hundred francs?' 'No,' said Monet, 'anything else you can have and welcome, but you refused me fifty for that and I would not let you have it for fifty thousand.'

It hangs still in the room at Giverny, delicate and evanescent, with its legend attaching to it, that was never forgotten, as letters from Clemenceau fifty years later prove.

There comes, however, always a turning point for the man who has not only genius but character. In 1880, when he was forty, Monet felt strong enough to hold a general exhibition of his work, old and new, in

the galleries belonging to the *Vie Moderne*, then owned
by the publisher Charpentier. Duret, in a preface to the
catalogue, claimed that Monet would take his place beside Corot, Rousseau and Courbet among the modern
masters of landscape. Yet the sales were negligible and
among the critics J. K. Huysmans, himself an inno-
vator, concluded that the Impressionists—and Monet
above all—had failed to give the public anything more
than crude and rudimentary sketches. But in 1881 he
revised his judgment and recognised that Monet's eye
'caught with surprising fidelity all the appearances of
light.' In that same year Clemenceau founded his paper
La Justice and chose as its art critic Gustave Geffroy.
Both these facts were of good augury for the painter.

Another quite different circumstance helped to bring
about the change for the better in Monet's life which
becomes marked at this time. Mme. Hoschedé, whom
he had come to know when her first husband was one
of his few purchasers, now joined her fortunes and her
family to his, while he still lived at Véthueil. Her four
children (three of them daughters), added to his two
boys, made such a household that although a recluse
from general society, he was only a solitary in the sense
that he lived and worked in little contact with his
fellow workers.

In 1883 the household moved to a new encampment,
and here at Giverny, to adapt the old Shakespearian
phrase, Claude Monet set up his rest.

CHAPTER VII

THE MOVE TO GIVERNY

IF WE agree that an artist's choice of abode is significant—and for a landscape painter it cannot be
otherwise, above all for one whose studio is the open
air—it becomes necessary to describe for English
readers the sort of country to which Monet was finally
drawn.

There had to be water; this already has been made
clear. Also increasingly with his maturity there was a
desire for seclusion. As a young man he accepted if
he did not seek out the companionship of comrades
struggling like himself to find out their way in art; he
had that company about him, or in easy reach, while
he lived at Asnières or Argenteuil. But the move to
Véthueil meant a separation, a plunge into the heart of
the country.

The Ile de France was the nucleus about which the
organised unity that we now call France grew and
consolidated itself; it was the birthplace of the
mediaeval architecture that all Europe owes to the
French genius; and even today its villages keep the
imprint of that feeling for beauty, which makes them
as natural and as gracious as the wild flowers in an

unspoilt countryside. For although the Ile de France is
to France what the home counties are to England, the
capital has not subjugated these rustic surroundings.
As far as Mantes, there is no doubt a large part of the
population whose daily business brings them to the
city; and quiet little hamlets have among their grouped
farmhouses dwellings that are used for summer holi-
days or week-end change. But the farmer dominates;
everywhere the business of the land goes on, and in
summer and autumn the whole face of the earth is
adorned with crops growing or crops harvested.

The character of the land from Paris through Normandy to the sea is high level downland, through
which the Seine has opened in ages past a vast winding
track, sometimes broad, sometimes narrow. To this
trench run down the gentle valleys with lesser water-
courses; and everywhere at the point where valley
passes to upland there is a fringe of wooding on the
steeper slope.

Véthueil lies about ten miles from Mantes, about
halfway by river to Vernon, which is the next important town after Mantes on the Seine's course to Rouen
and Le Havre. But neither road nor rail passes
Véthueil: the Seine here describes so deep a loop that
the way cuts across its base, and even today the only
public conveyance to the place is a local and very
countrified omnibus from Mantes. In the 'seventies it
must have been half a day's journey to get there from

Giverny seen from the Coteau

Paris. La Roche Guyon on the way to Vernon is even less accessible and even more obviously picturesque, perched on a high cliff above the river.

Monet painted here also; but the obviously picturesque was not what he needed. At Véthueil, it is true, he used more than once the church, set at the head of a great stair of broad stone steps, for the centre of a composition; but oftener he painted down by the river's bank, scenes of a few roughly built cottages with snow before them; or the river itself gradually bursting through a long expanse of ice. Many of them are melancholy pictures, and perhaps it is not fanciful to assign this to his prevailing mood in those years.

At all events, after a matter of six years working there, he left the place—most probably, I think, because it is hemmed in between cliff and river, and for freedom of movement and greater variety of subject he needed more open country. He found what he wanted near Vernon; close enough to an important town to be in reach of Paris, quite far enough from it to be undisturbed. Giverny is a couple of miles from Vernon, on the other side of the Seine. The rail and main road from Paris run opposite it, on the left bank, under a long steep curve of *coteau* closing the view on this side by a high wooded rampart. But on the right bank, the *coteau* slopes down gently and leaves a broad space between it and the river, along which runs a road having beside it a small branch rail. Giverny, when you came to it, was then a straggling line of houses all to the left of the road. Nowadays the geography is not so simple; the big tarred street, along which even some motor buses run, curves uphill towards the church and carries along at a higher level. It is called the Rue Monet. But the modest little narrow macadamised road with its railway embankment beside it is the Chemin du Roy, and still marks the limit of habitation; for all beyond is a huge stretch of land, dead level and often flooded in the winter.

The reason is that the river Epte, a considerable water, coming down from Gisors here meets the Seine, and before meeting it, is divided into three branches; and what is now rich pasture and cornland was once marsh and fen—a boundary between Ile de France and Normandy. Giverny, like Vernon (to which town it officially belongs), is across that frontier: and though not by blood, it seems to me that by upbringing and chosen surroundings Claude Monet must be counted a Norman.

The house which he found was a very simple farmhouse standing some fifty yards back from the road. Behind it began the cultivated slope of the *coteau*. In front was an orchard stretching out on each side of the central path that led from the road to the front door. This faced south, looking towards the wide level expanse beyond which the Seine's course was marked by the dark curve of wooded cliff. But between this and the house the view was obscured by a grove of poplars, following the line of the road in a stretch of swampy ground between the railway's embankment and a branch of the Epte. These were the materials out of which in a few years Claude Monet had made his garden.

It began with the orchard, which gradually from rough grass was turned into a garden packed full of flowers. Some of the fruit trees were kept, of course, not only or mainly for their fruit: Monet loved blossoming trees more than anything and if there were ever rarities in his garden, they were of flowering shrubs. Otherwise, what he sought after and attained was a bewildering profusion of colour, not grouped in large contrasting masses as the usage is in France, but scattered broadcast. My first impression of it was of a space so filled with flowers that you could hardly put your hand between them, and all of them common free-flowering things; an artist's garden not a horticulturist's: what is more, the garden of an artist who sought chiefly for the flicker and brilliance of innumerable tiny points, a general iridescence of colour: in short, a Monet picture.

The general effect was that of a wheatfield in which poppies and blue corncockles and yellow marguerites have run wild in confusion. But a scrutiny shows how the whole was planned—and planned by Claude Monet, for his daughter-in-law who now occupies the house keeps the garden, as he willed, just as it was when he and she managed it together.

Naturally it was a slow creation: pictures of his mark stages in its development: for instance, when he came, a path led up to the house between a row of small pines, and the flower-beds were arranged on each side of them. But these were soon taken away to make room for a succession of trellised arches which clambering roses would cover with innumerable bunches of light blossom. Monet never cared for big roses nor in general for big flowers; he wanted festoons, or upright regiments of brilliant little faces, throwing back the light of day in streams of pink or scarlet, blue or orange.

All the world can see this flowering garden of his, at a little distance; it is separated from the road by a low wall, surmounted by an iron railing, through which and through the broad gate of honest smithwork, all the world stares as it chooses. That is how I first began to be acquainted with it. Later, I learnt some local memories about these gates and palings. At the centre of the village, where an old road turns up along the nightingale-haunted valley that leads to the top of the *coteau* and the high downland, there is a café whose signboard reads *Au bon Maréchal*, 'The Honest Black-smith'. When Monet came to Giverny, the smithy was still working there, kept by an uncle of M. Jégou, who, now that there are few horses to be shod, has made it into a place to sit and drink in very acceptably —or for that matter, to stay in. This smith did all the ironwork for the garden and was on friendly terms with the Master. For one day when Monet, impatient over delays in the work, came grumbling and growling about *ces saligauds d'ouvriers*, the smith took off the cap from which a French artisan never parts, working, eating or drinking, and retorted, '*M. Monet, les saligauds d'ouvriers sont sous la casquette*': as who should say 'The man's a man for a' that'. A workman was not a dirty dog when he took his cap off. According to the story, though Monet's temper was not of the easiest, there was never a cross word between them after that.

At all events when this artist had money to spend, he spent it at his own door. Giverny remembers gratefully that he found it poor enough and left it prosperous; as his fame grew, other artists and people of taste followed him; for (except one disastrous villa) prosperity brought no ugliness to what is still a lovely village. Its old houses, even when they have been extended and modernised, are harmonious with the whole, just as the sun-dappled tiles (not red as in Burgundy, but soft brown and grey like a partridge's glossy wing) fall in with the gentle landscape.

Yet Giverny, even beautified as it has been, has only the kind of beauty which might be paralleled more or less in a score of other villages within a range of twenty miles; and even Monet's flower-garden, though I have seen nothing to touch it in France, and seldom in England, nor ever anywhere a display of flowers so stamped with the impress of a peculiar mind, still is not the wonder, the shrine which he made and kept for his worship of the beauty which irradiates the world. He loved his flower garden of course: Clemenceau, whose fierce life spent its last years embowered in roses, induced as if by magic to grow on the sand dunes of his house in Vendée—has told how Monet's first care every morning was to pay a visit to his flowers, go round them, touch them and caress them. But the other garden, unique and apart, was where he spent long days in absorbed contemplation before the central and final inspiration of his later life.

Monet's Flower Garden

CHAPTER VIII

THE WATER GARDEN

IT WAS a water garden. When Monet came to Giverny, he had the little branch of the Epte, swift-running in ripples, just beyond where his garden ended; half a mile off he had the Seine, which had flowed through all his life. But the Seine here was not, as at Argenteuil, mainly the crowded playground of pleasure boats, or as at Véthueil the highway for long strings of straining barges; though here also he painted its noble breadth with the *coteau* rising beyond and mirrored in its shining surface, or with the tower of Vernon's great church rising in the distance. Here at Giverny a great island, continuing the flat delta of the Epte, is cut off by a narrow arm of the Seine, hidden away by trees interlocking over it, the haunt of anglers in their punts, and of lazy pleasure excursions. He played with the water at first, kept a boat on it, and could slip down to it by his channel of the Epte, and he has painted again and again the stream under its green roof. But presently he wanted more—a piece of water of his own, to adorn after his own fashion; a mirror of the sky at his own door, to set in a frame of his own devising. So he bought the narrow strip of waste marshy land

that lay between the railway and the Epte opposite the
limits of his flower garden; he got leave to turn the
stream aside; and then in the ground among the
poplars where it had flowed, he set men digging out a
shallow pond with a sluice at the east end where water
could be taken in, and another at the west where it
could be let back again into the river bed. When the
pond was made he planted it with water lilies of many
colours. They were to be the central feature, the
culminating splendour when summer was at its height.
Yet since he was Claude Monet, the picture which he
set about creating in his water garden had for its essential, not flowers, but light; a mirror of the sky, decorated on its surface with the most beautiful lilies,
but holding also the reflection of those water-loving
trees which were to fence off this paradise from the
outer world. The pool as it is to-day is pear-shaped,
lying east and west with its broad end to the east
where the water is let in; and here was a grove of
poplars; they must have been ready to his hand, for to-
day they are eighty or a hundred feet high. Beside them
he planted ordinary upright willows, extending the
screen southwards to the flat expanse of meadow, and on
the north side between the water and the road. But on
this side also he set weeping willows to droop into the
water: and either his own pictures reproduced or the
photographs of the pool will show how superbly his
scheme justified itself. Even when the lilies are in

bloom, the willows' tresses make the picture as much as they. Another huge poplar was left to tower up where the pool originally ended. But ambition grew, and he dug further into the ground, so that he got his pear-shape; and where it tapered he threw across, raised in a high arch, a wooden Japanese bridge. Another weeping willow was set to droop over the water beyond the bridge: close to it was planted a thicket of bamboos; and under their delicate leafage ran the narrow outlet—as it were, the stem of the pear.

Beyond all this to the west, another grove of poplars shoots up into the sky. From a seat here you can look up under the arch of the bridge, with lilies on the water at your feet, along the whole stretch of water, dappled with lily blooms set on the broad glossy pads, olive-green mirrors on a mirror that had all the colour of the sky, with heaven knows how many other colours reflected among them.

Monet painted his pond from here in 1899; the picture, in the Tate Gallery, tells us when the lay-out of the pond was completed; but in truth he was never done working at it. Purists of horticulture would say that he spoilt its original perfection: that a water garden should offer to the eye only the things that naturally prefer a waterside. Nothing could be a more perfect setting for his lily pond than the enclosure of silvery-green leafage, poplar, willow and bamboo; nothing could vary more suitably and beautify the line of enclosing bank than the reeds, bulrushes and arrowheads which grow there in clumps, artfully disposed, and which run riot on the tiny island left in the broader part of the pond. Flag iris is there by right—a flower that Monet loved; in one of the Orangerie panels its tall shafts are seen as a yellow flame. Nobody need cavil at the blue amaryllis lilies which spring here and there from the grassy bank, and while the lilies are in bloom, add their vivid blue to the extraordinary mingling of colours on, or, as the eye sees them, under, the shining water.

But wistaria—that certainly has no waterside associations: yet Monet who cared nothing about purism and was gluttonous for colour wrapped and swathed his roofed bridge in a riot of the soft twining green which in spring would turn into a cloud of delicate lilac clusters. In one of his later pictures he has painted, characteristically, the bridge and its burden, and the lilac mist spreading and vanishing in the water below it.

More than this—worse than this, a purist would say —he fenced in this hidden garden with a high wire trellis and set rambler roses ramping over the whole of it. In June the little trains on that railway must brush past a hundred yards of pink blossom; and on the other side, towards the open meadow, where his domain was bounded by the Epte's rippling channel, two or three yards wide, a gravel path following the stream was all garlanded with roses overhead and on each side. They

Bridge and Willow Branches

come even into the central picture: opposite the weeping willows two benches are set facing each other, and over these is an arched pergola—smothered in roses. Monet painted that also, from across the water, with the gay pink reflections thrown in among the grave olive-green of the lily pads.

This picture, *Les Arceaux Fleuris*, was probably one of a series—forty-eight in it no less—shown together in 1909—all studies of the water garden executed in the quarter of a century since it began to be made. This was the last of such exhibitions, each bringing together many various 'impressions' of one subject, which mark his period at Giverny.

In every case, the individual pictures are scattered over the world; the poem cannot be read as a whole. Yet once, in his final effort, begun after his seventieth year, Claude Monet completed a group, conceived as a group, destined to be kept as a group; one more series —again pictures of the lily garden. But these, as all critics have seen, and no one so clearly as his closest friend Georges Clemenceau, are different in quality and almost different in kind from their forerunners.

In the work done before he was seventy, Monet's object was essentially to render what he saw. It never entered his mind that a painter's business was not to represent. Where he differed from other artists was that he endeavoured to see more, to represent not a generalised image of many passing phases, but actually one momentary phase of the illuminated world. In the later group, he let himself break loose from restrictions tying him to what he could actually see, and help to make others see; he painted, as it were, objects and light and shade caught up in a whirl of emotion. Water must be not less transparent, clouds not less airy, but more transparent, more vaporous: yet all exactness of representation is thrown aside. What he sees in his magic pool are not merely images but symbols. It is the cry of ecstatic contemplation.

In the end his concentration on this mirror of his, this model of his own creating, was such that people began to reproach him for looking at nothing but *un trou d'eau*. Yet although Clemenceau says with justice that he was a sedentary, and all the world knew him for a recluse, he has left evidence in plenty to show how wide-ranging was the curiosity of his eye, and it is necessary to recall the phases of it.

CHAPTER IX

SARGENT, GEFFROY AND BELLE-ISLE

A s soon as the means to move about were avail-able, Monet pushed out to far-off corners.

This did not happen at once, though the move to Giverny marks the turning point: letters of that very year, 1883, show that the whole of the artist group were desperately hard pressed. Pissarro writes that but for Caillebotte's assistance he could hardly have got through the summer; nevertheless he suggests to his friend that the manager of a *brasserie* at Montmartre will give him fifty francs for a decorative panel, as he had done to Pissarro himself, to Manet and others. The hint is to be passed on to Sisley. In short, any of them was thankful to know where to earn a couple of guineas. There was much scepticism as to the chances of a new venture in which Durand Ruel had engaged, on the advice of some American friends. Pictures of the group were to be sent to that year's exhibition in Boston. Nevertheless this proved to be the way of salvation. Miss Cassatt, who ranked as one of the group, had friends, no doubt, in the United States; but the man who did most to encourage America to buy the impressionists and above all to buy Claude Monet was John Sargent, now working in Paris, and swiftly recognising genius when he met it, with a judgment less dominated by tradition than was that of most artists in Monet's own country.

Sargent met him first about 1876, and jumped at the chance of knowing one whose art had as he says 'bowled him over'; and thereafter among all the French artists of that period, Monet was Sargent's closest friend. '*Mon cher Monet, je vous remercie et je vous aime*', the American painter writes in a familiar letter, dated in 1888. '*Comme artiste alors, je vous adore.*' Sargent had been buying a picture, the *Rocher à Tréport*, and describes how he sat in raptures before it,—although Monet, with his habitual growl over his own work, had said, 'I cannot share your admiration.'

It was a theory with Sargent that the reason why Monet's work so appealed to him—why it 'bowled him over'—was that both were astigmatic and saw the world in the same way. Later on, protesting against a friend's vague use of the terms impressionism and impressionist, he wrote:

'These words were coined in Paris at a particular moment when Claude Monet opened the eyes of a few people to certain phenomena of optics. . . . Not content with using his eyes to see what things were, or what they looked like, as everybody had done, he turned his attention to noting what took place on his own retina (as an oculist would test his own vision).'

In so far as this account implies that Monet proceeded on a theory, Monet himself denied it to Sir Evan Charteris. 'Impressionism is only direct sensation', he said. 'All great painters were less or more impressionists. It is mainly a question of instinct, and much simpler than Sargent thinks.'

But he went on to agree that impressionists had noted how strong light takes the colour out of tones; and that is why flowers look their best under a grey sky. Moreover he said, 'there is a *nuance* in the passage from one tone to another; for instance, between blue and yellow something happens which can be expressed in painting.'

In short all that Monet would own up to was that he had looked intently at the visible world and recorded what he saw there. But this is only a question of how he arrived at the result which Sargent sets down emphatically: 'Monet counts as having added a new perception to artists, as the man did who invented perspective.' Sargent accordingly preached the importance of impressionism to his countrymen in America; and he told them Monet was the head and front of impressionist art.

This decided people who had money to spend. Sales began and Monet slowly but steadily became freed from his embarrassments; he could extend his garden, and also he could move away from it to change of scene.

Almost every year's work now marked new discoveries: so early as 1885, in the International Artists Exhibition in Paris (where Sargent also exhibited) he was showing studies of the *Côte d'Azur*, near Menton and near Ventimiglia; and there were others brought back from his own Norman coast, at Etretat and at Pourville. Again and again he must have gone to this stretch of the Channel from Dieppe to Varangeville, whose old church he painted, as well as the queer gap in the cliff with its rude stairway down which bathers make their way to the sea. In 1887 Octave Mirbeau, a versatile man of letters and an enthralling talker who became one of the few habitués of the house at Giverny, wrote of Monet that he, alone of artists, had completely understood the sea; he alone rendered its shifting aspects, its colossal rhythm, the swing of it, the innumerable and endless play of light and its force, and even the very tang of its brine.

But by that time Monet had given proof of his power to render quite other scenes than the Channel with its shingle beaches and short choppy sea beating up against white and ochre-stained cliffs, or the blueness of the Mediterranean under sun and its grey under the mistral. He had made his own of a coast where seas are deeper and wilder and the coast-line more formidable than anywhere except on the West of Ireland. Geffroy opens his book with an account of their first meeting: it was at Belle-Isle-en-Mer, a rocky island off the Breton shore, meeting the full stress of Atlantic weather, wind and wave rolling from three thousand miles of ocean, to an unsheltered cliff-bound coast. At Kervillaouen, a hamlet under the lighthouse, on the very extreme point of all, Geffroy found quarters in a little tavern, and learnt that a painter also was staying there. The stranger appeared, sturdy, bearded, and dressed like one of the pilots of the coast with jersey and sea-boots. They shared a table. Monet, when asked if he was preparing a picture for the Salon, answered that he was not one of those whose works were sent there. Then, learning that his companion wrote on matters of art for *La Justice*, he greeted him at once by name. 'You have written on my work,' he said, 'and I thanked you already; I thank you again now.' So began an alliance which lasted forty years; only a few months divided the two deaths, and the younger man was the first to die. Geffroy was a link the more between Monet and Clemenceau. Probably indeed it was through Geffroy that the acquaintance of the *Quartier Latin* was renewed between men who had grown famous. After it had strengthened into indissoluble friendship, Geffroy was never excluded; and at his grave, as at Monet's, Clemenceau was the chief mourner.

In the Louvre a bust by Rodin gives us the scholarly sensitive bearded face of this critic who rendered so much service to beauty: it suggests also the quality of enthusiasm which marks his study of Monet. The book tells frankly with what delight and excitement he found himself established in that far-off fishing village, sharing life at close quarters with the great painter who had asserted his talent and maintained his convictions unshaken through all the disappointments of an artist's life, without yielding a jot before the unkindest mockery, or the admonitions of well-meaning amateurs or dealers, or the public's stolid ignorance, which now and then broke into malignant anger. One feels that Geffroy's impression of Monet always retained some trace of the storm-beaten, rugged surroundings in which they first met. The painter, faithful to his principle of direct study of nature, worked out of doors at Belle-Isle as elsewhere; often in sou'-wester and oilskins, with his easel moored by ropes to the rocks. He has left a portrait of his companion there, a Breton fisherman, bristly bearded and sea tanned: but in the pictures of the coast there is no trace of man; nothing but the wild crags rising in fantastic pinnacles from the lash of water, or the incredible Port Goulphar, a haven with cliffs all round it into which the water seems to make its way under an arch of rock.

This was a far cry from the lily pool at Giverny— yet seized and painted with the same passion of delight.

Monet's own account of that first meeting with

Geffroy is, naturally, less emotional and keeps a touch of his humour. When he settled into the tavern at Kervillaouen, his hostess asked if he liked lobster—'What a question,' he said, 'to put to a Parisian! Certainly, as much as you like, all the year round.' But after a fortnight of lobster for dinner daily and more lobster for supper, he began to feel that he could do with less of it; and when after the mutual recognition, Geffroy asked whether the painter had any objection to his sharing the lodging, Monet's answer was, 'Certainly: with all my heart stay here: but do you know the menu? Lobster.' 'Splendid, I love it.' 'Here's another, I thought to myself,' Monet adds, 'who will be cured of that passion.'

The artist probably minded hindrances by wind and weather more than privation of the excellent table, punctually served, which was part of his life at Giverny. But neither wind, weather nor even perpetual lobster could head him off the chase of a new subject.

artist knows these black hours and is unjust to his own talent. That is, he says, forgivable; but to scrape out canvases is criminal. And this friend gives the best consolation: he quotes what had been said by Rodin. The great sculptor had never seen the ocean till he came to stay with Mirbeau; then, 'I recognised it,' he said, 'from Monet's pictures'. They had given him the exact and vibrant sense.

This was written to a man of forty-six. Thirty years later, one finds it the chief task of Monet's friends to rouse up the artist, apparently so indomitable; they tell him to revolt against his own injustice of self-condemnation, and against the shrinkings of his own despair before the tasks that he himself had set.

Even when he was forty-six, by the judgment of his fellows his rank stood assured. In 1889 Rodin gave practical evidence of that esteem which Mirbeau had reported: he and Monet joined together for an exhibition of their work as a whole, bringing together examples of what each had done over a period of five-and-twenty years.

The two men were born, some say on the same day; some, that Monet's birthday in November 1840 was that of Rodin's baptism. It seems to me more significant that the same year France produced this pair of artists and also Georges Clemenceau. That was indeed a vintage: I doubt if any other European country in any year could match it; and not less remarkable than the extraordinary force of genius in these men was their vitality. All were close on sixty when writers throughout Europe, and French writers more especially, were announcing the decadence of France. Rodin had still the greatest of his work to do, though he was the least enduring among the three and died before he was eighty. As to the other two, all the world knows that Clemenceau only gave the full measure of himself after he was seventy-six; and if Clemenceau is right, the same is true of Claude Monet.

It is true, of course, that officially speaking neither Monet nor Rodin had obtained recognition by 1889: the display in that year of their work, held apart, was in a sense a challenging reply to their virtual exclusion from the great Exhibition which that year, among other pomps, celebrated the French Revolution's centenary. Nevertheless, a movement then set on foot shows Monet assuming leadership of the unofficial group and claiming for it the most decisive recognition. Manet while he lived had been its leading spirit; Manet had died in 1883, and there was no representation of his work in the public galleries of Paris. Claude Monet proposed to acquire by subscription among artists and men of letters one of his friend's most characteristic works, and present it to the State. The picture chosen was the *Olympia* which when exhibited had excited much angry comment. The name was classical, the nude lady who reclined on her couch was in no way

modelled on Greek lines. Manet had painted what
he saw, and had not troubled to consider how Praxiteles would have handled the subject.

Several of those who most admired Manet's work
and desired to see it publicly honoured and accessible,
yet wished that another picture had been chosen. They
felt probably that the painting represented not a nude
in the classic sense, but a modern woman divested of
the garments which she habitually wore. Undoubtedly
the choice did not make matters easier, but it was
never Claude Monet's habit to avoid difficulties.

At this time Antonin Proust, father of the novelist,
was Minister of the Beaux Arts. He was among those
who admitted that Manet should some day have his
place in the Louvre, and though he did not like the
Olympia he subscribed 600 francs towards the pur-
chase. By this time the press was on the alert, and
Proust explained to an interviewer that he had subscribed, knowing that the purchasers were chiefly concerned to assist Manet's widow; that they did not care
where the picture went and that he certainly would not
ask to have it admitted to the Louvre.

Monet was furious; he demanded from Geffroy 'a
good article' on the beauty of the picture and 'the
imbecility and rascality of certain personages.' Mean-
while he himself took the personage in hand. Proust
had said that it was treason to ask on behalf of Manet,
for Manet never asked anything for himself. Monet's

answer was that they asked nothing for anybody; they were offering the picture to the State. Because Proust did not like it, that was no reason why the State should refuse a gift whose value was attested by the names of the subscribers. The exchanges grew so angry that Proust issued a challenge, and Monet chose Geffroy and the other friendly critic, Theodore Duret, to act as his seconds. They arranged the quarrel peaceably (perhaps it is as well that Monet did not name Clemenceau).

Finally the picture was bought and accepted in 1890—for the Luxembourg: the Director of the Beaux Arts pointed out that the rule forbade the admission of any picture to the Louvre within ten years of its author's death. An understanding was reached that the picture should remain on view in the Luxembourg and not be sent to a provincial gallery. The end of the story did not come till 1906 when Clemenceau, after overthrowing a score of ministries, formed one himself. Monet going to Paris one day bethought him to call on the head of the Government and ask that *Olympia* should be transferred to her final station; and within three days the thing was done.

As early as 1890, when the project was started, Berthe Morisot, Manet's sister-in-law, wrote to Monet: 'You with your name and prestige are the only one who can force the gate open.' That marks the position he had attained.

Materially also it is significant that Monet could give a thousand francs; only half a dozen others subscribed so much (one of them being Sargent). Pissarro could only send fifty francs; Renoir at first said '*impossible de trouver de l'argent*', but later produced another fifty. Rodin with perfect dignity asked to be put down for twenty-five francs so that his name might be on the list. He was in a '*crise d'argent*' which allowed no more.

But essentially the whole episode proves that Monet's eminence, if not his pre-eminence, was fully established in the only world he cared for.

Monet's House at Giverny

CHAPTER XI

THE HAYSTACK SERIES

THE STORY of Monet's life is really the story of his paintings, and it would be impossible to exaggerate the concentration of his life on one purpose and one preoccupation. Yet he was too fully a man to abandon contact with the general movement of ideas; and Clemenceau insists on his love of reading. Moreover, the society which he valued was one in which general ideas had their full part. His group assembled monthly to dine together at the Café Riche. As has been said, Monet was anything but indifferent to the pleasures of the table, and in his own home he ate and drank with application, like a true Frenchman. No doubt the Café Riche did its best for celebrated guests, but the bill of company (to borrow a phrase of Swift's) was even better than the bill of fare. Pissarro, Renoir, Sisley and Caillebotte, of the painters, were regular attendants; de Bellio, a distinguished doctor, Roumanian by birth, and a good patron of the new school in art, was another. Théodore Duret and Octave Mirbeau, their champions in the press, brought a knowledge of many literatures—Mirbeau's memory is said to have been as encyclopædic as

Macaulay's; and sometimes Stéphane Mallarmé added his distinguished voice to the discussions. Geffroy, another habitué (Monet introduced him), says that these hard-working artists and men of letters took their pleasures gaily and even vociferously; battle raged, about art, literature, politics and philosophy. Renoir, whose intellectual culture did not go deep (his letters are as ungrammatical and slangy as a school-boy's), used, it seems, to hunt in encyclopædias for arguments to throw at Caillebotte, a genuine student, but with less talent for chaff. Mirbeau could talk down anybody, but (so I am told in Monet's circle) was never overbearing or a monopoliser of discourse.

And after it all, Monet could go back to his palette and brushes and the countryside where he belonged like one of his growing trees, living a life outwardly tranquil and full of delights, but also full of torments. So early as 1890 he was writing to Geffroy about his studies of water at Giverny:

'I've gone back again to things that are simply impossible; water, with the weeds of the bottom waving under it: marvellous to see, but to want to paint it is enough to drive one crazy. Still, this is the sort of thing I am always tackling.'

A month later comes the cry of one who persists in open-air study:

'I'm in the blackest depths and sick to the heart of paint-ing. It is an everlasting torture. Don't expect to see anything new. The little I've done is destroyed, scraped out and slashed to pieces. You don't allow for the frightful weather we have had these last two months. It's enough to make a man a raving lunatic, when he is trying to render the atmosphere, the whole look of things.

On the top of that, every kind of worry; and I'm stupidly afflicted with rheumatism. I'm paying for my standing out under rain and snow, and the heart-rending part of it is to think I must give up trying to face all weathers and work out of doors, except when it is fine. Life is a silly business.'

But several years later one of his excursions took him to Norway in midwinter and he writes to Geffroy, that he had been spending four days at a time in sledging through the snow over mountains and fjörds and lakes, and was delighted to find he could stand the cold better than the Norse themselves.

'I painted for part of today under snow falling that never stopped; you would have laughed to see me white all over and icicles hanging from my beard.'

One thing distressed him characteristically.

'I haven't been able to see a glimpse of sea or fresh water, all is frozen and covered with ice.'

To complete his impression of a country, Monet always craved for water—which is indeed everywhere in a landscape what the eye is to the face. But in 1890, turning away from his pools and impossible water-weeds, he carried out at Giverny the first of those series by which he is most fully characterised. In it there was no water to add its charm or its tormenting difficulties. He would show what the changing sky could make of a subject so simple as a haystack.

Once a young painter came to him (it is Mirbeau who tells the story) asking to be taken in as his pupil:

'I am not a professor of painting,' Monet answered. 'I only paint, and I assure you it takes me all my time. And I wash my own brushes. Besides, since the world was created, there has been only one teacher of painting'—and he pointed to the sky and its flooding light. 'Put your questions there, and see what answers you get. If you get none, then go into a lawyer's office and copy papers; it's an honest job and better than copying nymphs.'

But, Mirbeau adds, the young man had read art criticism and went off to a gentleman who explained to him the means of attaining to a *médaille d'honneur*.

So in 1890, with the sky for his guide, Claude Monet selected a suitable haystack in the field beside his house. Nowadays the new tarred road which is called Rue Monet cuts through there; but it was a big field then, sloping gradually from the level of the railroad up to the *coteau*, and lying fully exposed to the sun. He painted the haystack, the same haystack (a friendly farmer let it stay there as long as he wanted it) under full sunlight, seen through mist in sunlight,

Poplars by the Epte
Painted in 1894

seen at sunset, seen gray with snow on the ground, seen sunlit with snow, seen morning and evening, cloud or sunshine—sometimes with another stack introduced, sometimes with a background of willows, but essentially the same haystack under different illuminations. There was no more significant way of saying that the real person in a picture is the light.

After the haystacks came another series conceived and executed at Giverny. This time it was poplar trees—a line of them, or rather two lines at right angles to each other, tall straight stems and their leafage like banners in the sky. One of the series is in the Tate, and is reproduced here. 'What a real painter's work', Pissarro wrote—'and so decorative!'

Poplars have not a long life compared with other trees, and as the pictures show, they were ripe for felling when Monet took in hand to preserve their image. Still, I had the thought that they might be standing forty years later; but the facts are characteristic. They stood along the river towards the station at Giverny; and when Monet thought of his subject he knew that the trees were likely to come down. So he bought them standing. When the series was finished, another and a vainer man might have thought they should stay for a sort of monument: an Englishman might have thought, as so many Englishmen do, that it was a sin to fell a tree. But Monet, being French to the core of him, did as any other Frenchman would have

there is long transition. It is amazing how without exactitude of detailed drawing Monet contrives to convey the bulk and solidity of the mass and the profuse beauty of its detail. As Clemenceau says, the well-knit design brings out the geometrical plan of the whole structure and throws into relief the living vertebration of those intricate depths of sculptured ornament in which the statues are enshrined.

Yet here, though choosing for his subject a building that had resisted change through long centuries, Monet has once more chosen to portray momentary life. He paints, not the cathedral, but twenty phases in that process of the universe which from moment to moment is modifying not only the aspect but the very nature of the stone: he paints the cathedral answering as a flower or a tree answers to the caress or the onset of the light.

Clemenceau has given the picturesqueness of legend to some details of the artist's procedure. At Giverny, he says, when Monet was painting his haystacks, a wheelbarrow or even a farm cart was filled up with impedimenta, and a range of easels was set up in a field: as the light shifted, Monet ran from one easel to the other and went on with the successive effects. In prosaic fact, as Madame Blanche Monet affirms—with good right for it was often her function to push the barrow—machinery was not so complicated: one easel sufficed, but several canvases were taken to the field of action; and in essence the story is quite true. Each study could only be advanced in a certain condition of light; while that lasted, Monet worked, it is said, with extraordinary rapidity, putting on at arm's-length those touches whose effect could only be appreciated by standing back several yards, but which by some inner process he visualised in their result, as the deaf Beethoven combined those sounds which he could never hear. Then when an effect was carried as far as could be before the light changed, he passed on to the next and often wholly different attempt.

It is outside my purpose here to discuss this particular cathedral series of paintings. But in telling the story of Monet's life, and of this most notable among his friendships, surely it is worth noting what the two men meant to each other. Clemenceau's book is there to show how intimacy with the painter, and that intimate comprehension of the painter's work which companionship could foster, revealed to the man of action and man of letters new mysteries of beauty in the invisible world. Monet was doing for his friend what in reality his art sought to do for the world at large. Every artist utters first his own emotion, and seeks first the response from his own sensibility as listener or spectator, when the song or the picture emerges; but he seeks also the strengthening of that response in its reverberation from other minds. One may easily judge what it was worth to the artist, for

of Monet's life. Letters to Geffroy tell his attitude: his detestation for '*cet ignoble procès*', his growing admiration for Zolà's superb courage. Yet I think a man so secluded from all the contacts of public life might have stood aside but for this instinct to range himself beside the oldest of his friends, who was now the closest. He stood behind Clemenceau. Every one who took that side had to face fierce hatreds; the ease and well-being which had come to Monet so late in life was jeopardised; it was perhaps worse that friendships were threatened too, and not merely threatened. One of the foremost among those who had made the new group of painters, Degas, quarrelled at this time over the raging controversy with Claude Monet; they did not see or speak to each other for long years and then a common friend brought them together, counting on the link of a common calamity. He judged right: the two old painters, both threatened with blindness, ran to each other with the same cry: 'How are your eyes, Monet?' 'How are your eyes, Degas?'

Another characteristic trait of the man in this period is that when the Cross of the Legion of Honour was offered him in 1888, he refused it—though Rodin had accepted. His feeling on the matter was so marked that in 1900 Renoir, who in his turn had let himself be decorated, wrote at once hoping that this would not interfere with their old friendship. Another letter,

The Japanese Bridge, 1899

pathetically inconsequent, followed, apologising for the first. 'What can it matter to you whether I have a ribbon. You have always held your own way steadily, while I never could know one day what I would do the next. But you should know me better than I do, for I think I know you better than you do yourself.'

Monet thought presumably that if the State wished to show honour to artists it should do so, not by giving them ribbons but commissions; and the school of which he was the outstanding figure had received not the least official patronage. That no doubt hurt him. But as to the ribbon, Clemenceau says that whenever people asked Monet why he had no decoration, he used to chuckle contentedly into his great beard.

CHAPTER XIII

THE TEMPERAMENTAL ARTIST

THERE were great elements of the philosopher in this painter. Public applause did not concern him, he was well content with the verdict of the few who mattered—of Rodin, for instance, who wrote in 1897 that although both were so busy in pursuit of nature that friendship got little expression, he never failed in admiration for 'the artist who has helped me to understand the light, the clouds, the sea, the cathedrals.' These he said 'I loved well already, but your rendering showed me their beauty fresh awakened in the dawn.' Encouragement was not on one side only; Rodin was grateful for support when his Balzac received such a volley of abuse as recalled the time when it was 'the fashion to laugh at Monet's new notion of putting air into landscapes.' There are words of special praise from the sculptor for one of the haystack pictures: but the whole may be summed up in the signature of his last letter—'*Votre admirateur, A. Rodin.*'

Or again, the philosopher should be valiant against poverty, and Monet was certainly that; not flushed or intoxicated with prosperity, and here again Monet's discreet and sober use of money was philosophic:

self-sufficing, complete in himself, and above all reasonable,—except (it is Horace who adds) when he has a cold in the head. The exception as well as the general description holds good of Monet. Big trials he could stand like a hero, but the little ones flattened him out. In point of fact, what defeated him was denial of the indulgence for which he craved like an opium-smoker. While he could work, philosophy held out; but when the weather was too bad to work in, or when the results of working in bad weather tied him up with rheumatism, philosophy went by the board; he became convinced at once that it was a bad world, and that he was a worthless painter. There is a long letter from Octave Mirbeau remonstrating with this too quick despairer. Rheumatism was the matter, bad weather was the matter, and worst of all they had cut the weeds in the river he was painting. Anybody, Mirbeau said, was fully justified in cursing his luck. But to go on to the conclusion that he would never do work worth anything that year, or any other, was preposterous.

The real trouble, however, is touched on in Mirbeau's last sentence. 'You do wrong to complain: do not torment yourself by willing the impossible'. For in the very nature of things, a man who seeks in every picture to fix for ever one fleeting moment of beauty is doomed for ever to fall short of his desire. The very intensity of his effort condemned Monet to intensity of disappointment; but while effort could be renewed,

Haystacks, Late Summer
Painted in 1891

the remedy was there. It was only when something checked effort, and left the mind to compare results achieved with the thing aspired after, that philosophy went by the board.

But of course the man was passionate, and clung like a child to his treasures. Once a friend came upon him marching about his garden with countenance all broken up, the very picture of dismay. What was the matter? He would not answer, any more than a child will. What was it all about? Still no answer: until finally there came an outburst. 'Very well, I'll tell you. There was a storm yesterday. It killed two trees in my garden. Two trees, do you hear? It's not my garden now.' And he went on marching up and down muttering to himself. 'It isn't my garden now; it's not my garden.'

That is the story as Madame de Fels tells it; but if the storm was one that came in 1911, Monet really had cause for anguish. At the very centre of his water-garden was the pair of weeping willows planted close together so as to hang over the pool and so reflect themselves that the shallow sheet of water seemed to go down as deep as the trees were high. They must have been set there when the pond was first made, for they have a girth of nine feet now at shoulder high. That storm uprooted one of the two and flung it crashing through the rose trellis back on the little rail-

poet had brought Parisian ways with him to the heart of the country; Monet taught him to go to bed early and to get up fit to be a countryman; and he found himself vastly the better for this advice.

Yet from this very place the painter was writing to Geffroy for encouragement and moral support:

'My dear fellow,

I'm badly troubled, I've nearly lost heart and so tired that it has made me ill. I get nothing done that is any good, and in spite of all kind prophecies I'm afraid these attempts will lead nowhere. I never had such ill-luck with the weather; never three fitting days on end, so that I'm driven to continual changes, for everything is budding into green. And it was my dream to paint the Creuse as you and I saw it.

To make the story short, all these transformations keep me running after nature and never able to catch up; and then there is this river that falls and rises, one day green, the next yellow; half dry today, and tomorrow there will be a torrent after the desperate rain that is falling now. In short, I'm in great distress. Write to me, I want picking up badly, and you know yourself Rollinat is not the one to put me in form again. When I tell him my anxieties, all he can do is to go one better; and then, though he knows the difficulties of his own art, he has no notion of the trouble I must take to do what I do. All he sees in painting is the queerness of it.'

His first impressions had been of wild ravines in winter: especially of one old solitary twisted and terrible tree that stretched gnarled arms out over a torrent. Now that he wanted to paint it, this tough

The Willows that were Saved

old trunk began to put out green shoots; and Monet got villagers to come and clear away the green so that he could paint his picture,—to the vast amusement of the country-side. What capped the climax was that in his desire to save every moment, he got a barber to come and cut his hair as he worked in front of this wild subject—with Pistolet gravely mounting guard.

traffic, horse-traffic, traffic of railway engines, was a vast surge of life. Smoke wreathed up and blended with the fog, over the grey river, at this centre of a city whose life ran for the conduct of business; a strong outlet for the produce of these factory chimneys which he suggests against the dim horizon—for all that England had to carry overseas. The London that he feels and makes us feel is a seething and toiling centre of human effort. Traffic hustles along in a heavy jumble; but the scene has its own harmonies, for there also was the life of light. Geffroy tells how he and Clemenceau came to see the painter and found him at his window working upon a view almost invisible in the fog. Yet every now and then he would stop: 'The sun has gone,' he would say. For them the sun had never been there, and they looked out upon an almost featureless expanse in which the bridges and the river could just be dimly discerned. Suddenly Monet would pick up his palette and brushes, saying, 'The sun has come back.' They could see nothing of it: but gradually as they watched his work, their eyes learnt to distinguish a far-off mysterious light that seemed endeavouring to force its way into this dead world; and gradually in muted tones the hymn of light began to be sung.

There were thirty-seven of these studies when they came to be exhibited, in three groups: studies of Waterloo Bridge, of Charing Cross Bridge and of the

Houses of Parliament. For this last, essential in a different sense to the conception of London, Monet found a place to work on the other side of the river, somewhere in St. Thomas's Hospital; and he painted the square-topped tower rising high into the mist with flights of seagulls beating up through the waves of fog. No man who watches that central sketch of London River can miss the birds, always before the eye; and Monet may simply have seized on them for a decorative feature, as a Japanese artist would have done; for the art of Japan influenced him by a profound sympathy. But the pictorial impulse does not exclude other forms of the imagination, and he may well have had a thought not strictly pictorial in setting these symbols to flap and hover beside the majestic tower which in its own way symbolised and stood for the power whose essential dominion lay upon the seas. No flag, whatever its memories evoked, could be so eloquent.

The other series is far different. Few but this painter would have sought for beauty in the dim irradiation diffused through London fogs; Venice, on the other hand, was any man's enchantment. Monet went there for the first time in 1908, when he was close on seventy, fell in love with the marvel like a young poet, and wrote to Geffroy deploring that he had not been there sooner, when he was 'bold enough for anything'. Still, he said, the charm of the days he was passing made him almost forget he was an old man; and he hoped to come back another year and carry his studies to completion.

He went a second time and still it was not enough: he needed a longer period of close contact; but he could not get it. On both his visits Madame Monet had been his companion. After the second she died and as he said himself—'I could not face going back.'

He had to finish these pictures—which were shown together in 1912—from memory and from notes, working *de chic*—out of his head; and he was discontented with the result. 'I could do studies of Paris *de chic*,' he said, 'and no one but myself would find out. But Venice is another story.'

The difference must have been not only in the infinitely greater familiarity of everything in Paris. Venice rose out of water, with the flicker of light from it reflected on to the buildings, and the buildings themselves reflected back again. These were the things that even at Venice preoccupied Claude Monet; and some of his admirers, notably M. Camille Mauclair, found their allegiance to Venice prevail over their allegiance to Monet. They think he belittled the inherent splendour of buildings, in themselves perfect works of art, by regarding them chiefly as coloured masses to receive and give back the impact of light. Geffroy on the other hand chooses precisely this theme of Venice as a starting point for his view of Monet as the painter of all others least localised by temperament. He would have liked Monet to be perpetually a traveller that he might fix for us all the varied beauties of this globe; and for him this crumbling Venice seen hanging in a sort of radiant mist, as if across far-away centuries, is a vision truer to the essence than any precise detailed inventory either of its splendour or of its decay.

These variations of judgment are to be noted. But for my own personal feeling I can only say, to me Claude Monet seems to be most completely master of his subject when he is painting the scenes in which his life from boyhood to old age was mainly spent, the water by which he was nurtured. People spoke of him first as a sea painter; and Rodin thought that in Monet's work the sea found its completest interpretation. Yet in the sea pieces that I know of, which are mostly studies of the Channel, I find no more than is in many other artists' work; and the more grandiose effects of cliff and wave at war with each other which he found at Belle-Isle, do not seem to me more than bold suggestions.

Where his interpretation is magical and to me unapproachable is in those studies of his own great river to which, through all these years, he was continually adding. In 1896 a series of 'Mornings on the Seine' was exhibited; later there was a series of Véthueil; but when was he not painting these things? None of them is more typical than the study of the tranquil opening into the tree-roofed narrow waters of the little *bras* which strikes off at Giverny from the main river, la grande Seine, and comes out a mile farther west in the broad straight stretch which leads to Vernon.

Yet these are subjects common to a score or a hundred French artists. What belonged uniquely to Monet was the painting ground, studio and model at once, which he had created in his own garden and on which his effort was gradually concentrated, till at last all his endeavour was confined within the narrow space in which the painter's peculiar genius found such infinite horizons and so complex a world of colour and of form.

Branch of the Seine near Giverny at Sunrise

Painted in 1897

CHAPTER XV

MONET'S CULT OF LIGHT

So EARLY as 1899—we have the dated picture in the Tate Gallery for evidence—Monet was engaged in the effort to render on canvas aspects of the living picture which he had himself created. But during the next five years he was painting mornings on the Seine, scenes of the Norman coast and the Thames; and in each case studies accumulated over a succession of years. It was after the London series that he began to concentrate his effort on the bewildering beauty of a subject which lay at his own door. The group of pictures finally assembled for exhibition in the May of 1909 bore dates from 1904 to 1908. A few sentences written to Geffroy tell how absorbing was the work:

'These pictures of water and of reflections have become an obsession with me. The thing is beyond an old man's power, and still I want to succeed in rendering what I feel. I have destroyed some of them: I am beginning again on others—and my hope is that something may come out of so many efforts.'

There was no lack of response to his endeavour: the Nymphéas were acclaimed. Geffroy's book brings together some of the tributes; for instance, a letter from

work on the fields, to plow, sow or reap, herd the sheep or milk the cattle. More and more he loved scenes where only the wind and he had a free foot.

Others than he, thousands of others, have adored as he did the beauty of nature where it is alone, undisturbed by the presence of either man or beast. But on the whole, what nature-lovers for the most part seek out in such scenes is beauty of coloured form; and landscape painters, ever since landscape painting began, had been grouping on their canvas lovely combinations of form clothed in appropriate colour. Fidelity in representation was fidelity to forms, fidelity to colour. They knew, of course, that colour changed with every passing moment, but in practice they disregarded and minimised this inconvenience; a distant mountain should be blue, a cornfield golden, and so recognisable as such. Delineation had to be exact and characteristic. On the other hand, the landscape had to be lit somehow, but they conventionalised the light, choosing effects that made possible broad oppositions of light and shade.

The school of 1830, Corot and the rest, had come much nearer to observing the subtleties of a world lit from the vast sky; yet even they simplified matters for themselves by selecting those hours when nature is suffused rather than flooded with light. Grace of form they sought for and the delicate gradation of tones.

Monet's House at Giverny
Painted in 1912

Then came this young man, Claude Monet, in the strength and audacity of his youth, wanting to paint no less than full daylight. What was to them an inconvenience to be dodged and evaded, the dazzling brilliance of a perpetually shifting illumination, was to him the very essence of the beauty that he adored.

All phases of light, from the faint gleam of dawn to the far-off suggestion of sunlight struggling through a London fog, were part of his worship; but his art must face the sun in its strength in order to learn to contend with the cooler, the more evanescent, the delicately flushed tints. This nature-lover knew the face of nature as not even the trained eye of the country-bred knows it. A countryman, trained by experience and affection, is familiar with forms to a degree that is incomprehensible to the town-bred: he can distinguish a crow from a pigeon on the wing almost as far as sight reaches, just by the shape of the silhouette; he can pick out golden plover far off when they sit among the broken ploughland; can tell beech, elm or oak from each other by their outline far away; and so on. Probably Monet's eye was trained to note all this; but it was not such details that his painting suggested. What it shows is that he knew, as perhaps a shepherd knows, how a landscape alters at each hour of each day, but with far keener sensitiveness to all gradations of the change. And the landscape painting that he set out to make was concerned less with form than with the changing beauty imposed by light upon permanent form.

As his art developed, as his contemplation was prolonged, form itself grew less stable to his gaze, less exactly outlined. His incredible concentration of eyesight showed him that to the eye things do not precisely define themselves; there is in nature no hard and fast line to be seen; beyond all the curves and undulation, from the boldest to the most delicate and exquisite, there hangs a kind of flickering aura, bridging the transition to some other surface that gives back the light. Form with him grew less and less precise.

Yet when he represented solid objects, since their solidity and the quality of it were part of life, his eye and hand never avoided the essential. His cathedral, emerging from the mists, seems not less weighty, not less huge than other men's, but rather the more immovable, the more cliff-like. His cliffs have all the strength of rock. In a picture that adorns a London house there is a study by him of the Manne-Porte near Etretat, a projecting nose of the cliff under which the wave has made passage, behind a rib of rock, forming a natural arch. He has painted with delighted observation all the variations of the light as it streams through towards the side in shadow which is next him; he has tried to catch the brilliance of it through the spray where waves break at the base of the arch's column; but at the same time, no one can look at his picture and not feel at once the lightness and the strength of that natural buttress, so curved that it might have been designed by an engineer to resist the outward pressure of the vast weight of clay and rock which it supports.

Or again, in the same collection is a most lovable sea piece, somewhere off that same coast; sunlight, and on sea-water, barely rippled yet showing the set of the tide. A couple of boats are on the water and the boats are painted by a man who has the feeling for a boat and knowledge of its build and handling.

All such work of his can be reproduced with some appearance of adequacy in black and white; the more important the decorative aspect of his design (as for instance on his poplar studies), the less it loses in transference from colour. Even his haystacks can be very tolerably photographed and do at least suggest the picture, because the nature of the object emphasises the distribution into light and shade, no matter how deliberately Monet graded the transition. For that matter, there is included among the illustrations to this book, a picture whose title is *Les Coquelicots*—the poppy field. Needless to say, in the photograph all this essential feature is lost completely; Monet's handling conveyed poppies as a sheet of diffused colour, and no trace of poppies can be found here. But the picture

represents so well the *coteau* behind Giverny, the movement of the ground, the whole aspect of the countryside, that I put it here as giving what is not and cannot
be registered in the direct photographs of that same
landscape.

Still, when all is said, pictures of the impressionist
school lend themselves less to reproduction by photography or by engraving than the work of any of their
predecessors, because in their effort to catch light as it
is in nature, they shunned those managed oppositions
which had been previously in vogue; and also because they thought less and less of form. And of all
the impressionists, Monet is the most difficult to
reproduce, the one who sacrifices most to truth of
actual daylight; who refuses most absolutely to represent objects and scenes as the public had grown used
through centuries to see them represented, by artists
adopting a convention for which good reasons could
be pleaded. Yet he is nowhere else so impossibly difficult as in the studies of his culminating period, when
he shunned solid form increasingly, and made his
picture out of a surface of water, with only a few lily
plants scattered on it to mark the planes. On the
water, on the flowers and their leaves (other mirrors),
light streamed down; and below the water, as it
seemed, deep masses of foliage or delicate cloud
vapours fused imperceptibly into each other, yet kept
their characteristic outline. Through colour he must

express this delicate impalpable, almost formless world; and when colour is taken away, nothing remains in these pictures but the summary design of lily pads, beautifully spaced and ordered, with some indication—it cannot be more—of the subtle gradations of light where the only shade seen is among the reflections.

across long meadows to the rampart of trees which mark where the Seine swings its wide curve. Yet there is not here, what I think must be felt even in the least adequate reproductions of Monet's own impressions —the dreaming mind, the rapt contemplation, and the potent touch, caressing that image of loveliness, outlining, indicating rather than drawing, the modelled masses of coloured light about the lily patches.

This does not apply to the painting in the Tate, which really does not belong to the group. In 1899, as I conceive it, Claude Monet was so enchanted with the garden, then newly come to perfection, that he painted it almost leaf by leaf, showing the profusion of blossoms he could reckon, while under them the water showed dense with green herbage reflected. As compared with the later work this is the prose of the garden; it is seen almost as any garden-lover might see it. Like all this artist's pictures, it needs to be viewed from a long distance; judging by my observation, half the people who stop before it cannot have a notion of its effect. But at the proper distance, look at the small spaces of open water (in those days the lily plants were less spread out) and observe how limpid is the water's translucency: ask yourself by what magic you can actually see, though you cannot trace, the sheeny film of it between you and the greenery of those reflections.

Everything is there in this picture: trees and the reflections of them, plants on the bank and their image also; it is crowded with green life. Few painters have been so little afraid of a green picture as this lover of the sap of life.

In the group exhibited in 1909, there is far more selection; a motive is chosen from the garden, it does not now sit for its picture. But still, when the selection has been made, the artist's aim is to convey what he feels by direct representation of what he sees. If all those lily pictures were available together, nobody, I think, would want to get photographs of the water garden. Yet since all of them are scattered, it would be possible only to collect photographs of these, a poor substitute indeed.

But I think that the direct photographs and a few reproductions, however inadequate, of the later paintings, may help to give some idea of the garden that Monet created and of the way in which its beauty appealed to him, before he used it in the last years of his life as a theme and inspiration on which to build up in its praise a poem complete in all its parts.

I am never likely to forget the shock of first encountering what was to me a new discovery—reached under the happiest conditions. For beyond all doubt the ideal way to make a first contact with Monet's house is to get there by water. Wandering about, I had taken Vernon as a centre for exploration and somehow became aware that Claude Monet's garden was at

Giverny, a little way off, and should be visited. Since the weather was glorious summer, and all Vernon heavy with the scent of lime blossom (the town has four kilometres of avenues of pleached limes) I suggested that river would be better than road.

From the boat-slip, which is fully a kilometre from the bridge at Vernon, it was, I was told, four kilometres against the current to Giverny if I went by the main river (*la grande Seine*); but a side channel gave an easier journey for canoes. The young lady who arranged the letting thought my skiff would not get through; but the boy at the landing-stage had more confidence, provided I looked out for stumps.

It was a tight fit, and the stumps were many and not all self-evident; the big willow trees met overhead, letting in shafts of sunlight on quiet stretches, where anglers watched their floats among the arrow-headed weeds; but it was an enchanting way of approach, and at the end of half an hour we emerged on the main river. A picnic party on the bank showed us where Giverny was; nestling along the foot of the *coteau*, it looks south across a fertile expanse of cornland to the line of poplars bordering the river and to the wooded cliffs beyond it. Following a field path, we reached a rippling little stream—one of the several branches into which the Epte divides before it falls into the Seine.

Across the stream was an old road marked Chemin du Roy; but a lane took us into the modern tarred

A Poppyfield at Giverny
Painted in 1885

motorway, and its name was the rue Monet. Along it
we strolled, looking, if truth must be told, for a place
of drinks: yet not too thirsty to observe perhaps a
score of grey-roofed farmhouses, looking like things
that had grown out of the ground, or into it. Artists
who have colonised here deserve the credit. The village
church, too, had a broad simplicity of lines, and, like all
else there, it spread out laterally; nothing in Giverny
is pointed, nothing is cramped, the world has elbow
room.

Where we got drinks, we were told how to find
Monet's garden, and the directions took us back to
the Chemin du Roy. On our left was a low wall topped
by a long iron grille, perfectly simple in design;
through it one saw a long, low farmhouse, having in
front of it a dazzle of flowers, all common, all chosen
for their brilliancy: snapdragon, African marigold,
campanula, gladiolus and the like. What struck me at
once was that there was no arrangement in masses.
The painter had his garden before him like a canvas
some fifty yards wide and rather more than half as
deep; and the effect he aimed at was an effect of the
whole. All was a flicker of bright colour; form was
given by the use of trees, limes, conifers, and one or
two Japanese maples, crimson or bronze. Looking
close, one could see careful planning; common willow
herb had been brought in for its tall shafts of clear
colour; they were ranged in clumps at intervals;

nothing was let stray, yet the whole effect seemed as carelessly variegated as a wheat field where poppies and blue corn cockle have scattered themselves. All fell together like a pheasant's plumage or a peacock's; and, remembering how many colours this master had found in the shimmering warmth of a sunlit haystack, one could feel a little what he was after in creating that ordered space of vibrant light and life; how he must have, watching the whole as a whole, picked out the innumerable notes that merged into its harmony.

We turned back to go; and across the road and the little rail beside it was another grille which gave a glimpse of water shining under willow trees, and of crimson water-lilies. But it was only a glimpse, and we did not guess the luck that was in store; yet, though we thought we had seen our last of Giverny, we were well content with what it had given us. Sculling back, this time by the Grande Seine, beauty was everywhere about us; the long, sinuous recession of chalky cliffs reminded one that, after all, neither Monet nor any other French painter had so caught their vaporous loveliness as one cross, niggardly old Englishman; and that day of sun and great white flying clouds had all Turner's airy lightness. Two kingfishers that flashed out on us as we skirted the big island put the final touch to delight.

Next day we had to leave soon after lunch, but there was time to find a photographer who might give at least some aid to memory. I found him, a little fat man, made up to resemble Gambetta. Whether his black beard came from the Midi or no, he had all the southern expansiveness, and told me with sympathy and regret that I asked the impossible. The Master had no tolerance for photography and no camera was allowed in the garden. But he said M. Butler, his son-in-law, an artist himself, who had charge of the Master's testamentary dispositions, was the most charming of men. 'I will go,' I said, 'and ask M. Butler if I cannot get a photograph of a picture of the garden; for surely it has been painted many times.'

A taxi brought us to where M. Butler was living in a house of his own in the painters' colony at Giverny; and I found him an American after the type of Henry James, which is another way of saying what the photographer had told me. He put us in charge of his son— also a painter—who escorted us to the farmhouse and presented us to the Master's daughter-in-law, who is the garden's real custodian. She received us in a great room hung with canvases finished and unfinished, and with the most perfect graciousness confirmed what we had been told. Then I made my suggestion. But, she said, nobody except Monet himself had painted in the garden; and what he had painted there was in the Orangerie at Paris. She had certain photographs of these famous panels; and while she went to look for them, we were studying a portrait that stood on the table; and the artist who had taken it was no less a man than Sacha Guitry. The Master was wearing his eighty years as if they weighed no more on him than the vast beard which swept over his big chest. France, I think, produces the finest old men in Europe. At all events, this was an Olympian—so mellow, so strong, so genial, so comprehending a face I have never seen.

We explored the flower garden, this time from within the railing; and then our guide led us across the road into the other close. It was a far bigger stretch of water than I had guessed, bright and clear; the little branch of the Epte runs beside it and can always be turned in to freshen it. But the flowers for which it was put there like standing water; and they were suited evidently to their hearts' desire. Under the spread of a vast weeping willow, and beyond it, patches of water-lilies, crimson, pink, cream colour, white and lemon yellow, spread their glossy leaves over the surface. Here, again, all seemed haphazard, yet all was design; each group was held to its appointed place and not allowed to merge into its neighbour nor to encroach too far upon the willow's mirror.

There were other trees, of course, all round, and shrubs and winding walks led through them; at the west end, where the water narrowed, a bridge spanning it was smothered in wistaria—in July, of course, only a mass of tender green, but think of it earlier! Yet the essential of that garden was the exquisite drooping of delicate boughs above and the upturned faces of those strongly modelled blossoms, each crying out its colour. That was the beauty that everyone could see. Colour photography could have reproduced something to recall it. But what is painted at the Orangerie gives not what the rest of us see, but what Monet saw through it: the quintessence of that beauty, not the form and colour only, but the vibration, the palpitating life that brought the whole into one harmony. A Chinese painter said (so Laurence Binyon tells us) that if your subject is a pear tree in blossom, it is not a pear tree you have to paint; you must paint the dance of the soul of a pear tree. Claude Monet has left his garden for others that come after to see; but he has left also at the Orangerie what he went down by the water on summer days and summer nights to look at—the dance of the soul of his water garden.

CHAPTER XVII

FROM YOUTH TO AGE

Monet's life in its period from fifty years old onwards must have been like a rich autumn. Sir Evan Charteris in his *Life of Sargent* has given us a sketch of the painter as he looked even in extreme old age, only a few months before he died:

'The activity of his compact frame, the vigour of his voice and the alertness of his mind pointed to an astonishing discrepancy between constitution and age. He struck a visitor as at once gay and kindly, keen in his wit and emphatic in his prejudices, wholly simple and unaffected, with something rustic in his bearing. No one could have failed to notice the touch of dandyism visible in the cuffs of ruffled lawn which projected from the sleeves of his rough summer clothes, nor the fineness of his hands, nor the curious quality of his eye which, magnified behind the lens of powerful spectacles, seemed to possess some of the properties of a searchlight and be ready to seize the innermost secrets of a visible world.'

If that was the man at eighty-six, half-blind and spectacled, what must he have been, thirty years, even twenty years earlier, approaching the grand climacteric, or only just past it. All was well about him. The material difficulties were surmounted; he was free from cares of money, free to work unharassed by those interruptions which fret the inmost fibre. But free from the cares and even the torments proper to his nature, he was not nor could ever be. Even now when the rewards of his long battle began to pour in, he relaxed nothing of his effort, for it was life itself to him; followed up for its own sake, for the joy of it, but always beset by its own affliction; always, when judged by his own standards, falling short.

Yet if such existence is not happiness, it is hard to know where happiness should be found. He had the means now, when the eye and brain were jaded, to change his scene and renew them by the stimulus of novel beauty; and while he stayed at home, he need not stint himself in the delight of decorating still further and maintaining in perfection the beauty that he had made. Half a dozen gardeners were kept at work on that little domain of two or three acres; and over and above his flowers he had other luxuries for his eyes, peacocks, pheasants of all colours, glossy plumaged ducks, and at one time several seagulls that a friend had picked up wounded, and sent to be Monet's pensioners.

The little farmhouse was enlarged, with no great change in its appearance; what was long and low originally, grew longer at each end; but addition was made in such a way that the big room, which served as Monet's studio when work must be done indoors,

A Border in Monet's Garden with Willowherb and Marigolds

should still have a window to the west as well as two facing due south on to the garden. Wherever he lived he must have light in plenty; he hated darkness. Here in this room, when his work was done for the day, he would put it in front of him, and sit for hours at a time in concentration on it, considering where it failed, how it could be amended. For the eye, his special faculty, did its work under the direction of thought constantly applied at all times, and not only face to face with the subject. The hand also learnt in advance what it had to do, and the combination was planned by which splashes and streaks of the most un-likely colours would come together at the proper dis-tance and represent, say, the trunk of a tree with its living quality.

But if the man lived in seclusion it was anything but solitude. Faces and voices were many about him and the house had to grow to make room. He brought to Giverny his two sons by Camille; Madame Monet brought four children of her first marriage. Geffroy recalls how full of young life the *salon-atelier* was when he went there for the first time in 1886 and how wel-coming a hostess was Madame Monet, providing the best of cheer for her guests, and leaving them every freedom for talk.

As the young grew up, there were marriages; all three daughters left the home. Mr. Butler, the American artist who had joined the colony at Giverny, did not take his bride far. But in 1899 this daughter's death was a first blow to all the happiness.—In 1911, when Madame Monet died, the old man's house was left to him desolate. They had been over thirty years together and had come through hardship together into prosperity. How much the companionship stood for, one does not know; but stray allusions in the letters show that she was fully interested in the work of such men as Rodin, and that Monet depended on her to keep him in touch with Geffroy when he himself did not write. That appears from a letter in 1908 when she had gone with him to Venice. She went again the next year; and then came her illness. Monet would not go back to Venice without her, not even for the sake of completing to his satisfaction work on which two long periods of study had been employed.

Early in 1914 came a new bereavement, the death of his elder son. Yet, in a sense, for him good came of evil. Jean Monet had married Blanche Hoschedé, one of the children of Madame Monet's first marriage, so that Monet's step-daughter became also his daughter-in-law. This daughter now came back to the house in which she had grown up, and in which she had learnt to be herself a considerable artist. For the rest of Claude Monet's life he had the support of this care and this companionship.

Clemenceau also was near by in these years, having

settled himself not far from Gisors, some twenty miles distant along the valley of the Epte; always eager to render the best service possible to such a friend, always urging him on with that work which was the man's whole life.

So far back as 1895 he had expressed the regret that no one was found rich enough and wise enough to acquire one of the subject groups in its completeness, for the sake of those who, seeing only one single movement of the painted symphony, could not arrive at the full meaning of the whole. The instance which he chose then was that of the haystack series, which illustrated to him art's progress in the perception and comprehension of light. Fourteen years later when the forty-eight Nymphéas were brought together in 1909, a critic (Louis de Fourcaud), writing in the *Gaulois*, took up the same cry. The tiny lake, he said, was in itself a creation, a work of art, in which the powers of nature had been guided to display themselves in a restricted field, but within it had full and free play.

'We are face to face with something unexpected yet longed for, made of the very stuff of dreams, yet absolutely real. The lily pond, all diapered with their corollas, has horizons like some legendary sea, and more mirages than words could suggest. Perfect harmony breathes from the radiant whole, full of lovely life and steeped in tender silence. The eye cannot tear itself away. I cannot think without melancholy how these enchanting creations, which together are a single composition, must so soon be scattered. Once only, and for a little time, they will have been assembled to convey the whole scope and purpose of the poem which is built up through them. Never again and nowhere shall they be seen grouped as we see them: they will be gone to the four corners of the world, exquisite fragments, yet each revealing only part of the secret that is in all of them. Assuredly we would desire that they should be preserved in their completeness in the hall of some palace where we might be admitted to see them decorating their resting place with a splendour and a serenity peculiar to themselves.'

Monet himself must have thought of all this often and often; Clemenceau, no less surely, from the very nature of their relation, must have kept the thought before him. Work he must, in obedience to that craving for expression and for realisation of a vision which all his life had obeyed. Money need not be thought of; and there was no reason why he should not attempt another theme, in which the structural unity of the whole should be essential; a group of paintings expressly designed to remain together as a group, each completing each.

There was, however, an agonising impediment. The superb faculty of nature which had both permitted and enabled the peculiar application of his brush was now failing. Sitting where he had sat so endlessly, before a subject so infinitely familiar in its changing beauty, he found that colour lost its old brilliancy, and that he could no longer distinguish the fine gradations of tone. He, of whom a critic had said that he had cleansed the eyesight of all painters, and taught them to see clear in the light, now found that the freshness had faded from his palette. He set the new work beside the old, saw the dulness in it, and fell on the unhappy canvas with his pocket knife. All the comfort doctors could give, was that cataract takes years to develop, and that even for the chance of operation he must wait and wait.

He could not wait, inactively. Trying his hand in sketches innumerable, he discovered that although the detailed study of near objects, and the play of light on them, now became impossible, he could yet see well enough, as well as ever, for the setting of vivid isolated points of colour against sombre masses of tone. He must generalise. He could no longer represent the world as it had been his delight to behold it, his torment to try and reproduce it, with the quivering flicker of actual day over all, animating all. He must paint now less directly from vision, more from accumulated knowledge. Inevitably then these later pictures come more from the inner than the outward vision; they were such stuff as dreams were made of. 'Your young men shall see visions and your old men shall dream dreams.'

Pourville, so that the recession of chalky cliff serpentines away eastward till the broad white streak narrows down almost to vanishing; and the curve makes an enchanting lazy pattern across the canvas beyond the blue-green sea, in which, though it has not the milky look familiar on the Kentish coast, the chalk somehow affects and tones down the blueness. It is a picture of diffused sunlight, high summer in a heat haze; exquisite in colour, not less exquisite in composition, and of absolute truth to the scene, which is rendered with a touch that never for an instant suggests roughness or effort of any kind.

Perhaps no one else could have painted it; Boudin's studies of that coast are as true, but they have none of the power, the large, broad-shouldered swinging rhythm, that is always characteristic of Monet's design. For that matter, Boudin's truth is always generalised; it is never so completely as in this canvas of Monet's the presentment, not of a day, but of an hour, clothing the landscape with a vesture luminous that never exactly repeats itself or is renewed: the vesture of one moment in the eternal ebb and flow of light.

Yet the scene so painted is one that revives for any of us memory of what we ourselves have seen; we are guided insensibly and unawares to a beauty that for ourselves, though perhaps never in such fulness, would have been revealed to us. What Monet painted in the Orangerie is what none of us has seen or will see;

something built up out of common vision by intense contemplation; a beauty beyond the surface beauty, with the essentials of it rarefied, intensified and woven together into a fabric of the dreaming mind.

Something is gone; much is gone; youth is gone—youth that adored broad daylight. The film that lay over the painter's eye is over the canvas; colour has not the old purity. Monet himself was never at ease about these paintings. His old age was haunted by a dread of leaving work that should misrepresent him, and one day a friend came in and saw great volumes of smoke rising from the garden. 'What is it,' he said, 'a fire?' 'Yes,' said Monet, 'a big fire. Come and see.' The pile was heaped up with smouldering canvases. He had remembered how often after other men's death there was a rush to gather up the least fragments left remaining, and he chose to destroy while he still lived whatever he did not wish to survive him.

His standards were terribly exacting. It is great odds that but for Clemenceau the nymphæas of the Orangerie would have gone into another bonfire, because they had in them the defects of his aged vision. The world, I think, is Clemenceau's debtor for this—and for all his dealings with Claude Monet.

CHAPTER XVIII

CLEMENCEAU AND THE NYMPHÉAS

IT WAS in 1914 that Monet finally decided to carry out the work which had planned itself in his brain as a complete composition; each subject holding its place in the total grouping. He saw his way, even with the decaying machinery of sight that was now at his disposal.

He would paint in several panels from different standpoints the entire circuit of his pond. The work was to be on a scale larger than ever he had undertaken, even when his young audacity tackled twenty-foot canvases for his *Déjeuner sur l'Herbe* or *Femmes au Jardin*. For this venture a studio was needed of size to match; a barn forty foot wide by seventy long, and fifty in height. The date fixed for beginning the construction was of all days in the calendar, August 1st in that fated year.

Inevitably, building could not go on. But Monet was not to be stopped from his purpose by a European war—in which his surviving son was of course engaged. He continued his studies for the panels, he got workmen and material as and when he could. By 1916 the studio was ready, and he ordered canvases to be stretched, seven foot high and fifteen broad: forty or fifty of them. These were set up on wheeled easels and ranged in a vast oval round the studio; for his decorative plan involved a place for display that should be either circular or, by preference, oval—after the fashion of his pond.

Then he set to work, with steadily deteriorating eye-sight, and all the agony of self-depreciation that was his torment: 'the luxury,' Clemenceau writes, 'that complete achievement permits itself.' Yet the canvases grew, filled with Monet's vision of still water, carrying on its surface a few score of flowers at their live anchorage, but reflecting in the compass of a stone's-throw the immeasurable sky. The sensation was not of daylight, for only in this watery reflection was the sky seen; it was a world half real, half shadowy; the picture of a pageant in which trees, flowers, earth, water and the great sky took their part, and in which the mirrored image was always a live emanation, as real as that from which it proceeded. Yet throughout, even when object and reflection seemed almost fused, one never lost the sense that the actors in his pageant were of two spheres; one never ceased to feel the more immediate, more assertive vitality of those strong flowers whose long supple tubes draw up at once their sustenance from water and from soil; whose life requires the constant presence in full measure of two elements to maintain the solid sculptured beauty of blossom and of leaf.

Only now and then the bank was seen with its leafage; now and then, to establish the planes and buttress up the structure, willow trunks made a bold line from top to bottom. In other panels, the pendent branches drooped across, like fingers from an unseen place reaching downwards for some exquisite contact. But essentially it was a water pageant, all in blues shading to mauves, and green shading to grey or olive; though here and there was the rosy reflection of a cloud spreading, and in one panel, the earliest of the year, a yellow flame of flag-iris above the water and re-flected in it. Except for this, only the lilies made strong points of vivid colour; and they too, like the flag iris, were seen simply as colour patches, not drawn in their detail; yet the difference in their life was there.

How much was done in this seclusion while the war stormed and thundered, I cannot say. But here the only storm was in the artist's unquiet mind, perpetually driven forward, perpetually tormented with failure. At last out of doors, beyond the garden close, the war ended; armistice was signed; and Georges Clemenceau, who for two years had been at the helm of France in hurricane weather, had a day to take his rest. The way that he chose to spend it tells more than volumes about the man and the nation he stood for. Others went for quiet to their homes, their churches, their golf courses: Clemenceau came down to Giverny, taking Geffroy with him, to decide which among the canvases round the walls of Monet's studio should be chosen, as the painter's offering to France in honour of victory.

The project must have been discussed often between the two old men (they were both close on seventy-eight); for except the nation there could be no fit recipient for that gift and there was no one but the artist to decide its destination. Yet certainly till that day Monet had wavered uncertain; but on that day it was not easy for any Frenchman to refuse Georges Clemenceau anything.

I cannot hope by any description to give any adequate idea of Monet's pictures in the Orangerie— though I must try later on to say something more about them. I cannot produce photographs which give even a faint impression of their quality. But it should be possible to make English readers understand how much is implied in Georges Clemenceau's choice of that day's occupation.

If ever a nation knew a supreme moment, it was France in those first hours of deliverance by victory. If ever a man had the right to feel that he stood for and spoke for his nation, it was Clemenceau when victory was won. When he came that day asking, it was France that asked. Yet he chose that day to make his request definitive because he knew that it would be irresistible and he knew that obstacles had to be broken down. He had to conquer the diffidence of a great artist.

One of Monet's Studies of the Nymphaeas,
Painted in 1904

The French have a noble concern for things of the mind, things that build up the intellectual life of a nation. None had this more than Clemenceau; and he was bent on securing for his nation what he counted a supreme treasure. But bound up with the treasure was his friend's glory. Nothing was nearer to his heart than the lifework of this friend which he had watched developing through now more than twenty years of close intimacy. He loved beauty and this was to him a new revelation of beauty, the more enthralling because it was new and difficult. It was a presentment of the visible world, still strange to thousands, a revelation which this friend of his, this man of genius, was gradually making familiar; and it was his pride to be near the work, to act as its interpreter. For long years Monet had known contumely; when success came, it had no hall-mark of the nation set upon it; and it was now in Clemenceau's power to set that stamp, coming to Monet with a request which was the supremest tribute, that he should bestow upon the nation the culminating harvest of his immense labour. That this gesture for which he asked should have a touch of reprisals, made it the fitter to please Georges Clemenceau. For fifty years of the artist's working life the French State, which regularly and habitually buys the work of living artists to furnish its museums up and down the country, had never bought one canvas from Claude Monet; and when he applied to be entrusted with public commissions he had been rejected for lesser men. Now the answer was to be that, when all the world was ready to clutch at Monet's work, the neglected man should give to his nation the most important work of all: not a thing to hang in a corner, but the full decoration for two vast halls. The man who spoke for France was inviting this Frenchman, this friend of his, to disregard with a sort of Olympian disdain all the official judgment implied in France's attitude during half a century.

The difficulty to be met in Monet's opposition was indeed one of humility, yet of a special sort. A lesser man, in whom vanity was master, could not have done other than accept (with suitably modest declarations) such a tribute as was offered in the request. But the artist's most intimate and most honourable pride rose up in alarm. To give in such a way, with such pomp of circumstance, meant absolute assurance; and never till his death was he assured that this work of his was good enough to be so given. It is not that he doubted of his title to be included among the French modern masters; a generation earlier he had fought passionately for Manet's admission to the Louvre, and he could not but know and feel that where Manet was, he had the right to be. But this new work of his, this complete poem of the garden, was different in quality, almost different in kind, from that by which, in his own judgment, he had attained to mastery: it lacked, for nature now denied them to him, attributes which to him had seemed essential. The supreme clarity of vision, the skill to note and render every flicker of living light, belonged to an earlier period. Was he going, he must have asked himself, to let his life's work be represented by things done in his decay?

But Clemenceau insisted, urging by word of mouth that passionate conviction which runs through all his book on Monet—and it is agreed that neither in his writing nor in his public speech was Clemenceau's fascination comparable to what it was in his familiar talk. To him, the work of Monet's age surpassed that of his prime; faculties had been liberated, ranges of brooding thought and imagination, which were held in leash while brain and hand were on the strain to record exactly that momentary dazzle of phenomena in which Monet's eye sought its delight of living beauty. There was in Clemenceau a natural prepossession which it would be stupid to ignore. At the age of seventy-six Claude Monet entered into possession of the great *atelier* where these pictures were to be achieved. At the age of seventy-six, a few months later, Clemenceau entered upon control of France in her struggle for life and victory. By the consent of all, it was only after the age of seventy-six that Clemenceau had given the full measure of his powers. He had shown that, where will and brain retain their vigour, the weight of accumulated experience and long-gathered thought may be worth more, to the man who can handle it, than faculties of the prime. It was like him to believe that another man also in old age might outdo all his earlier achievement.

He was not the only one, by many, to see in Claude Monet an indomitable prowess; and one poet fixed that feeling in stanzas like sculptured marble. Henri de Regnier calls up in line after line all the revelations that had sprung from Monet's brush; light playing upon haystacks, on cathedrals, on the vastness of the sea and the vastness of the forest; night's approach, day's dawning; the great river winding its slow courses, the meadow-land spread out under gentle sun; rocks sun-baked, burning shingle; dawn and noon, morning and evening, wind and light made palpable, and the face of earth grave and pure under its snowy mantle. He calls up a thousand canvases, trophies of a thousand efforts; and at the end of all, he shows us a man seated quietly by the lily garden where the flower-studded water dreams under the sky; a man wooed to new effort by every image redoubled there in the pool where every broad lily leaf seemed to offer a palette.

'For,' the poem ends, 'neither time nor strain, nor glory, nor age, nor all that immense labour had wearied the artist's hand; adventure still beckoned:'

> '*Et pour vous, O Monet! le plus beau paysage,*
> *Sera toujours celui que vous peindrez demain.*'

In January 1921 a collection representing Monet's work over fifty years was shown in Paris. The *Nymphéa* group of 1920-1921 was included, and they were received with acclamation. This no doubt helped the final resolve, but still more decisive was Clemenceau's return in March from shooting other tigers in the Indian jungle. On a day in April 1921 there was an assemblage at a notary's office in Vernon, and before distinguished witnesses Claude Monet signed a formal donation of the Nymphéas to the State. Conditions had been laid down; they were to be permanently housed in a building constructed to the design he had planned; they were to be placed and displayed in the order which he indicated. All the terms were accepted; yet when he signed the document tears ran down his cheeks. 'It is great arrogance to make such a gift. What will the people say who come after me?'

That doubt never left him. Once before, in a black mood, he had wanted to burn them, but Clemenceau stopped him, saying, 'You can't do that: you are pledged.' Now it was made irrevocable; but he refused to let them go while he lived and could still endeavour to bring them nearer to his conception. Clemenceau and the others about him could only stand by and tremble for the result; Clemenceau above all had to try and cure the self-tormenting mentality.

But first it should be set down here that not only the

149

a bad judge of your judgment and that it is a folly to begin again on a completed work.'

So it went on. Nothing broke the friendship; but the Monet that Clemenceau knew was very different from the calm Olympian of Guitry's photograph or the ardent, gentle contemplative that Renoir had painted forty years before. To Clemenceau, the artist was completely expressed in that passionate self-portrait which is on the wall at the entrance to the Orangerie; an old face suffused with excitement; triumphant as if from possession of the dream realised; congested with effort, but the deep-set eyes glowing and jubilant as they dart out their glance from under the pent-house of bushy brow and from all the converging wrinkles that tell of effort concentrated with superhuman intensity on the act of sight.

Gradually the painter's strong life flickered out. A letter reproduced in facsimile by Clemenceau shows in the wavering of the hand more than its words say of the doctor's verdict.

When Monet died on December 5th, 1926, with his family about him, Clemenceau also was there. When he was buried, by his own wish, simply as a peasant, Clemenceau stood by the grave and said nothing. But, going back to his shelter in La Vendée he found that he had still words to say. The last labour of his life was his book on Claude Monet and the Nymphéas.

CHAPTER XIX

VALEDICTORY

IT IS strange to have written so much of torments besetting one whose life seemed an idyll of peace; to whom success had brought full measure of every reward; whose very work was in itself delightful, whose last labour was to renew in another medium mirrors of the serenest beauty.

Yet in truth, of the two old men whom it is impossible to separate in this reconstruction of a life, I believe that far less anguish and anxiety came to the one whose existence had been spent in strife; whose supreme effort was the direction of a struggle into which men were battered into mud and bloody pulp, while behind the lines, at the directing centre, feuds, jealousies, ambitions and exacerbations of anger raged like wild beasts. The other life, seemingly of peaceful contemplation and loving service to beauty, was solitary, shut up in itself, endlessly self-questioning. It was spent in contemplation, not pursued as an end in itself, but under the perpetual urge to wrest utterance out of that silence: to fix for ever the vision of an hour, or a moment. And the torment was measured by the

curled up slightly when they touched the water so that each became a little boat, poop and prow complete, adrift on a tiny voyage till it reached some lily harbour. He would have watched, as I did, a brood of young swallows perched on dry branches of a willow waiting while their mother came and went, returning to poise skilfully to drop the morsel into the nearest open beak till one youngster, feeling neglected, took wing too, hovered midway and intercepted the ration. Above all, the old artist must have seen scores of times, as I did once, a kingfisher flash past, vanish, and then suddenly, almost from over my shoulder, cross the pond in a stretch so short that his arrowy flight must be checked, and one had the rarest view of lapis lazuli on the wing, but flashing as no stone ever flashed.

On every sunny day that he spent there Monet was in the centre of one of his own masterpieces, a creation so happily come to the birth that it was no wonder it should in itself become in its hour a creator—the inspirer of a less perishable beauty. Nothing that his hand and eye unaided could make might ever rival what he had perfected in unison with nature; earth, air and water conspiring with him year after year to bring to birth the deliberate splendour of this planned and ordered beauty.

Yet these living pictures are fragile. Another storm

may shatter the willow group less retrievably: a couple of seasons' neglect, and the lily garden would be overrun, if only with lilies: for their toilette must be made like any lady's, dead flowers cleared away, the superfluous leaves removed so that each plant may spread out its group of broad palettes level and shining: and but for constant rakings, weeds from the bottom would choke the whole.

What will last, at least for centuries, is the reflection of the water in the strange and bewildering mirror of Claude Monet's imagination, fixed on canvas by the indefatigable prowess of his hand and eye.

Everybody will interpret these canvases in his own way; I set down merely a few notes. One is of a different season from the others, that in the first room with a flame of yellow flag-iris—seen, as the lilies are seen, without attempt to model their form. There are as yet no lily flowers: reeds shooting up from the water help the design. This panel seems different from the rest: the painting of the water and leaves to the right of it is absolutely perfect representation, but to the left the reflection of a heavy pink cloud is not vaporised, and the transition here is not happily given. On the whole there is in this room more direct representation: it is here you get the suggestion of depth in the water from the willows' reflection, and there is incredible lightness given to their trailing branches which hang down. The picture which faces one on entering is frankly portrayal: the hour is evening, the lilies are shut, the plants seem to hang as if in the air, belonging to a different medium from that in which the reflections have their being.

In the second room, all purpose of detailed representation is abandoned: at the end is the longest of all the panels, fifty feet long, curving round the end of the oval; and it is really a kind of dream of lily plants floating upon rosy vapours of cloud. Yet one can see in this, and that to the left, that it is a morning picture with light slanting in from the left: in the third, where the pond is viewed from between willow trunks close to the eye, full sunlight pours down, centring on a group of crimson lilies set among the innumerable sparklings of water just touched by the wind.

And as you look the branches of the willow between you and the sun actually seem to sway.

The last picture of all shows dusk coming on, with thunderous purples of storm cloud; and the willow tree shakes down dark tresses as if it were night in person.

The full length of the room is none too far a range from which to view these works: those which must be seen across the narrow of the oval suffer, I think, from the nearness. But at proper distance it is incredible what delicacies and subtleties are attained by this painting with its huge brush strokes. Across the room, one sees the willow trunks stand up solid and massive, apparently uniform in tone, yet somehow round and living. Go near and you see that they are powerfully modelled with great slabs of bright colour.

But people must see for themselves and feel for themselves. I think, however, they will feel more if they realise where and under what conditions these things were done, and what relation they bear to the vast industry of Monet's life: that these are in truth the dreams of a poet painter, inspired by the water garden which he had himself created, and which came to be a sort of divining crystal for his old age.

At all events Georges Clemenceau had his way. Claude Monet is represented there at the heart of the splendours of Paris—and represented by that which in Clemenceau's judgment was the most characteristic expression of Claude Monet's genius. Only for Clemenceau, these panels would probably never have been completed, or else would have been destroyed by Monet in his rage for perfection. Only for Clemenceau they would certainly never have been established as they are in the Orangerie.

He has recorded his own feeling that the presence of these works was little known: and I have reason to believe that this is still true. Within the past two years there have been in the other galleries of the

Orangerie temporary exhibitions of the work of Monet's comrades and fellow-workers—Manet in 1932, Renoir in 1933. Yet many who visited these exhibitions never knew that another doorway in the same building led to this collection of paintings by the head and front of the Impressionist school. This book will have been of some service if it makes English-speaking visitors to Paris aware of what they otherwise might miss.

How great an artist Monet was it is not within my competence to judge. But beauty as he felt it and rendered it was a thing remote from prettiness. It had a tidal volume, it was an aspect of the universal flow. It had the majesty of the great river which one may say flowed through all his life. To my apprehension, at least, there is in all his work a vibration deeper and stronger than in that of any of his fellow-workers.

As to the man himself, we have Georges Clemenceau's estimate. Those who make themselves familiar with the vigour, the versatility and the scope of a book written by its author in his eighty-seventh year will understand why other appreciation seems an impertinence. It is true that Clemenceau was writing of a man he loved: not less true, that Clemenceau's mordant intelligence had been for seventy years in intercourse, friendly or more often hostile, with all that was most notable in France. He was not one to whom eulogy

Looking towards the Coteau behind Giverny

came easily. Yet on leaving Claude Monet's grave, he found himself driven by the impulse to 'speak with sincerity of what he felt, what he saw, and what he loved in a great figure that had passed away'. What impressed him was 'the spectacle of a human life completely devoted to ideal purposes by an irrepressible outflow of enthusiasm, directed and controlled by continuous action of the will'. And the man whose life afforded this spectacle was in Clemenceau's judgment ' an honour to his age, to his country, and to the planet on which he was born'.

These are high words indeed, but it was no common nature from which under the stimulus of bereavement there comes so challenging a cry.

The garden at Giverny will be to me not only a memory of the rarest beauty that I have beheld and the most perfect adaptation of nature to a work of art; it will be remembered not only as the inspiration and birthplace of many exquisite works; I shall always think of it as the quiet corner in which two old Frenchmen, full of years and glory, who had no single attribute in common but genius and indomitable courage, walked together as friends.

APPENDIX

THE FOLLOWING works by Monet are publicly accessible in English-speaking countries :

At the Tate, there are three connected with Giverny.

Nymphéas: seen under the Japanese bridge, 1899. (This is referred to in my text.)

Poplars—one of the series referred to : the foliage dark against the sky which is a heavy blue. But another artist, who had painted at Giverny for a while, described to me precisely the charm of looking up at the poplars and the preternatural blueness of sky so seen. This was said without any reference to this or any other Monet picture.

Landscape (bought from Monet by Sargent) is, I think, a study of Giverny; the church vaguely seen through a grove of young poplar trees, which are leafless: their trunks show almost mauve or lilac against the intense green of grass: and the feeling of spring's approach is in the clear thin air.

There is also the study of a lady sitting on a bench in a park, tree-shadowed, with sunlight streaming through. And there is the lovely picture of Rouen Cathedral, with its west front catching the evening glow high up while the rest is in blue twilight.

An example of his early work (dated 1870) is the *Beach at Trouville*; two ladies sitting with sunshades. The influence of Manet is strong in the characterisation of the figures; but the essential concern of the picture is to show how the light plays on them: it is the active part of the picture, not, as in the lovely Boudin close to it, simply a condition of the day.

On the opposite wall is the picture of Véthueil under sunshine and snow referred to in my text; it has beside it, or almost beside it, admirable landscapes by Sisley, by Pissarro and by Boudin; yet it seems to have a stir of life in it which they do not attain. It is living light.

This picture is part of Sir Hugh Lane's bequest which by an unsigned codicil in his will was left to the Municipal Gallery in Dublin; and Lane's admitted intention will no doubt some day be honoured.

The Courtauld Institute at 20, Portman Square, accessible every day to art students, and to the general public on Saturday afternoons, has two Monets: a flower painting, and one of his studies of the Seine, early work dated 1872, with a certain coarseness in the handling of autumn-coloured trees and their reflections on the left: whereas the tree group and reflections on the right are exquisitely gradated.

In Dublin the National Gallery of Ireland has

Seen through the Willow Branches

another river landscape, painted much later, with exaggeration of the broad strokes of pure colour juxtaposed.

The scene is, I think, on the main river, opposite Giverny, with the bank of trees fringing the long island, and the tower of Vernon seen in the distance.

The Municipal Gallery possesses one of the London series, and one of the best (Lane bought it); its effect is all in heavy purples and greys; the crowded jostle on the bridge, and the factory chimneys beyond it carry out the suggestion of a congested life.

The National Gallery of Scotland has one of the Poplar series.

The National Gallery of Canada has one of the studies of Waterloo Bridge, seen in a fog.

But America is much richer than the British Commonwealth in works of this master.

In New York. At the Metropolitan Museum:

> *Apple Trees in Blossom.*
> *Landscape.*
> *Norman Coast.*
> *A Field of Poppies.*
> *London: Waterloo Bridge.*
> *Landscape.*
> *Antibes.*
> *Needle Rock, Etretat.*

Havemeyer Collection:

> *The Green Wave*, 1865.
>
> *La Grenouillère*, 1869.
>
> *Sunflowers*, 1882.
>
> *Chrysanthemums*, 1882.
>
> *Poplars*, 1891.
>
> *Haystacks*, 1891.
>
> *Les Glaçons*, 1892 (a gift to Mr. Havemeyer).
>
> *Bridge over Lily Pond*, 1899.

Boston. Museum of Fine Arts:

> *Marine—Boat at Anchor.*
>
> *The Cliffs at les Petites Dalles* (Norman coast, 1880).
>
> *La Débâcle à Véthueil*, 1880.
>
> *Flower Beds at Véthueil*, 1880.
>
> *Sea-coast at Trouville*, 1881.
>
> *Ravine of the Creuse*, 1889.
>
> *Bras de Seine near Giverny*, 1897.
>
> *Nymphéas*, 1907.
>
> *The Grand Canal, Venice*, 1908.

Chicago:

> *Cliffs at Trouville*, 1896.

Pittsburg. Carnegie Institute:

> *Nymphéas.*

Worcester. Art Gallery:

> *London: Waterloo Bridge.*
>
> *Nymphéas.*

INDEX

Bazille, impressionist painter, 20, 26

Boudin, painter, 11, 12, 25-26, 38-39, 136, 138

Brasserie des Martyrs, 14-15

Butler, M., 125, 131

Café Riche, meeting place of the group, 81

Caillebotte, painter, 41-43, 67, 82

Camille (Madame Claude Monet), portraits of, 23, 24, 33; death of, 41

Cassatt, Miss, American artist, 42, 67

Castagnary, critic, 40

Cézanne, Paul, 23, 37, 48

Charteris, Sir Evan, vii, 69; his sketch of Monet at 86, 129

Claretie, critic, 40

Clemenceau, Georges, *Claude Monet, Les Nymphéas*, vii, 4, 65, 89, 162-163; the *Nymphéas* bequest, 4, 5, 139, 143-154, 155-156, 161; 26-27, 51, 60, 65, 71, 76-77, 79, 87-89, 132-133; relations with Monet, 89-90, 134, 145; the Dreyfus episode, 90-92.

Corot, 11, 14

Courbet, Gustave, 23, 25

Dame à la Robe Verte, La, 23-24, 33

Daubigny, 5, 13, 14-15; in London, 30-32

Degas, 39, 48, 92

Déjeuner sur l'Herbe, 21-22

Dreyfus, Captain, 90-92

Duranty, critic, 48

Duret, critic, 32, 40, 48, 51

Faure, singer and art patron, 50

Fels, Mme de, vii, 48

Femmes au Jardin, Les, 24

Flower garden at Giverny, 1, 3, 6, 7, 57-60, 123-124, 130-131

Forain, 48

Fourcaud, Louis de, critic, 133-134

Geffroy, Gustave, Monet's biographer, vii, 15; meeting with Monet at Belle-Isle, 70-73; 79, 82; with Monet in the Creuse, 99; 106-107, 109, 132

Giverny, description of, 6-7, 55-56, 122-123

Guitry, Sacha, 4, 126

Gleyre's studio, 19, 45

Haystack series, The, 83-85, 88, 133

Hoschedé, Mme (*see* Madame Claude Monet)

Houssaye, Arsène, critic, 23

Huysmans, J. K., 51

Ile de France, character of, 53-54

Impressionism, literature of, vii; and the public, 7, 37-42; a northern movement, 33, 34; Monet's definition of, 69, 111

Impressionists, school of, 23-24; origin of the name, 37; 40; names of, 48; Monet's leadership of, 66; success in America, 67-68; criticism of, 48-49; 1874 exhibition of, 38-40

Jongkind, critic, 16, 20, 25, 26

INDEX

PRINTED IN GREAT BRITAIN
BY ROBERT MACLEHOSE AND CO. LTD.
THE UNIVERSITY PRESS, GLASGOW